FORGED
in the
FIERY FURNACE

Forged
in the
Fiery Furnace

African American Spirituality

DIANA L. HAYES

ORBIS BOOKS

Maryknoll, New York 10545

Founded in 1970, Orbis Books endeavors to publish works that enlighten the mind, nourish the spirit, and challenge the conscience. The publishing arm of the Maryknoll Fathers and Brothers, Orbis seeks to explore the global dimensions of the Christian faith and mission, to invite dialogue with diverse cultures and religious traditions, and to serve the cause of reconciliation and peace. The books published reflect the views of their authors and do not represent the official position of the Maryknoll Society. To learn more about Maryknoll and Orbis Books, please visit our website at www.maryknollsociety.org.

"My People" from THE COLLECTED POEMS OF LANGSTON HUGHES by Langston Hughes, edited by Arnold Rampersad with David Roessel, Associate Editor, copyright © 1994 by the Estate of Langston Hughes. Used by permission of Alfred A. Knopf, a division of Random House, Inc.

Published by Orbis Books, Maryknoll, New York 10545–0302.

Manufactured in the United States of America.

Manuscript editing and typesetting by Joan Weber Laflamme.

Library of Congress Cataloging-in-Publication Data

Hayes, Diana L.
    Forged in the fiery furnace : African American spirituality / Diana L. Hayes.
        p. cm.
    Includes bibliographical references (p.   ) and index.
    ISBN 978–1–57075–472–2 (pbk.)
    1. African Americans—Religion. 2. Spirituality—United States. I. Title.
    BR563.N4H3788 2012
    248.089'96073—dc23

                                                      2011037787

For all of my students,
past and present,
young and old.
I have learned so much from you.
I hope you learned a little from me,

and

For my brother-in-law,
Craig M. Pitches (1955–2011),
who was always interested in everything,
and left us much too soon.

Contents

Acknowledgments

This book would not have been possible without the patience and able assistance of Robert Ellsberg and Susan Perry, editors at Orbis Books. Robert, especially, kept encouraging me when I would have to write and say that the project had to be postponed once again because of my ongoing health problems. It is absolutely joyous finally to have finished this long overdue work. The added time did however give me the opportunity to do even more research and have access to books and authors that had not been published as recently as last year. Their work has enabled me to explore spirituality from a Black perspective even more deeply than I had originally planned.

I also wish to thank all of those who listened to and commented on my many lectures and speeches about Black spirituality, especially my students of the last twenty-three years at Georgetown University who raised intriguing and challenging questions that forced me to again dig deeply into the Black historical experience in the United States. I dedicate this work to them.

The past decade has been very difficult for me as I have struggled with increasing health problems and numerous hospitalizations. I thank all of those who called and wrote and sent cards, especially my Grail and womanist sisters who encouraged me to keep writing and lecturing when and as I could. You helped me to realize I was not alone in my suffering and, as with Black Americans down through the ages, helped me to affirm that what does not kill us most definitely makes us stronger!

Introduction

Forged in the Fiery Furnace

Upon the hard rock of racial, social and economic exploitation and injustice black Americans forged and nurtured a culture: they formed and maintained kinship networks, made love, raised and socialized children, built a religion, and created a rich expressive culture in which they articulated their feelings and hopes and dreams.
—LAWRENCE W. LEVINE[1]

The people now known as African Americans[2] came to the United States in diverse ways, some directly from Africa as indentured servants or slaves, and others by way of "seasoning"[3] in the Caribbean islands of Santo Domingo, Cuba, or Jamaica. Some few came as free Africans to help colonize and settle the newfound land in company with their European brothers and sisters. However they came, they did not come empty; they carried on their backs, in their minds, and within their souls the richness and texture of lives lived for generations in towns and villages in West and Central Africa.

The heritage they brought with them provided the foundation for their development as a new people with African roots but, over time, uniquely American branches. The worldview, traditions, stories, musicality, and religious beliefs of their African ancestors were preserved, completely in some cases, partially in others, built upon, syncretized with new understandings

1

and ideas, and passed down from generation to generation, mother to son, father to daughter.

Despite what has historically been claimed regarding the negative impact that the Middle Passage[4] and slavery had upon Africans in the United States, those enslaved were able to retain and maintain many aspects of their African heritage, which enabled them to withstand the trauma of enslavement. In the words of historian Lawrence W. Levine, "Even in the midst of the brutalities and injustices of the antebellum and post-bellum racial systems black men and women were able to find the means to sustain a far greater degree of self pride and group cohesion than the system they lived under ever intended for them to be able to do."[5]

African American spirituality was forged in the fiery furnace of slavery in the United States. The ore was African in origin, in worldview, in culture, and in traditions. The coals were laid in the bowels of ships named, ironically, after Jesus and the Christian virtues, which carried untold numbers of Africans to the Americas. The fire was stoked on the "seasoning" islands of the Caribbean or the "breeding" plantations of the South where men, women, and children of Africa were systematically and efficiently reduced to beasts of burden and items of private property. Yet those who came forth from these fires were not what they seemed. Despite the oppressive and ungodly forces applied against them, they forged a spirituality that encouraged hope and sustained faith, which enabled them to build communities of love and trust and to persevere in their persistent efforts to be the free men and women they had been created to be.

African American spirituality is a result of the encounter of a particular people with their God. It is their response to God's action in their history in ways that revealed to them the meaning of God and that provided them with an understanding of themselves as beings created by God. Thus, African American spirituality cannot be understood without the knowledge and understanding of who African Americans are, how they came into being, and why they have somehow been able to grow, develop, mature, and persevere as a people of faith in the face of seemingly insurmountable odds.

The African American spiritual story is one of hope in the face of despair, of quiet determination in the face of myriad obstacles, of a quiet yet fierce dignity over against the denial of their very humanity. Theirs is a spiritual history literally written in the blood, sweat, and tears of countless foremothers and forefathers who died under the lash, were sold as commodities, were treated as less than human beings, but who struggled and survived despite and in spite of all forces arrayed against them. It is the story of their encounter with Jesus Christ who enabled them to find a "way out of no way," who justified their self-understanding as children of God, and who enabled them to persist in the belief that one day they would be free.

The spirituality of African Americans expresses a hands-on, down-to-earth belief that God saw them as human beings created in God's own image and likeness and intended them to be a free people. It is a spirituality that is often seen as typical of the Old Testament in its emphasis on justice but also of the New Testament in its emphasis on community and liberation. This means that God is a God of justice and judgment who rights all wrongs and condemns wrongdoing, yet that same God is a God of justice and love who promises salvation, both here and in the hereafter, to all who believe.

It is a contemplative, holistic, joyful, and communitarian spirituality.[6] This means that it is expressed in prayer through a deeply conscious prayer life that is not passive. Unlike in the Western tradition, there is no separation between the sacred and secular worlds; instead, they are interwoven and lived as one holistic way of being in the world. African American spirituality also calls forth the joy of loving God and acknowledges receiving the grace of God in song, story, dance, and other expressive and emotion-filled ways. It is also communitarian in that it helps to weave together a community of those who are connected not merely by kinship or blood ties but by ties of shared oppression and denigration of their humanity. This community is revealed both in worship and in other activities that give life to the community.

Lastly, African American spirituality is grounded in a devotion to the Holy Spirit and her ability to create possibility in the face of denial. The Holy Spirit sustains and nurtures the African American community, enabling it to express its joy in myriad ways that reveal the interconnectedness of God and humanity in a world graced by God but stained by sin.

African American spirituality is a tapestry woven with tired but expressive hands, hands that are crooked, torn, and bloodied from their heavy toil yet soft and gentle as they caress those they love. It is crafted from the stories of Africa, peoples and places unseen but remembered with fierce pride and savage joy, giving strength to bent and weary backs and heavy-laden arms. It is the song of a mother rocking her newborn to sleep in a grass-roofed hut, echoed by a mother in a tarpaper shack, both seeing the future in their child's sleep-heavy eyes. African American spirituality is the moaning cry of a man worked near to death yet determined to carry on for the sake of his mother, his child, his wife, his people. It is the gathered souls of a people torn from their native land, crushed together on filthy, plague-ridden ships, and hauled ashore to be separated and sold as beasts of burden and objects of sexual pleasure to people claiming the name of Christian.

African American spirituality is born of the pride and the pain, the horror and the hope of a people whose eyes have always been watching God and whose hands stayed firm on the plow as they fought their way to freedom. It is a spirituality forged in the fiery furnace of more than four hundred years of slavery, segregation, and racism but grounded in a history thousands of years old of a people who believed in someone greater than themselves and who, as a result of that belief, built civilizations and cities, raised families and created communities, gave birth to leaders and warriors, and passed on their hope to those who came long after them in a different land and facing far different circumstances. Theirs is a spirituality that emerges from and is sustained by their love of God, love of self, and love of each other long before they heard of Jesus' Great Commandment. This spirituality sustained and nurtured them and enabled them to hold their heads up and "keep on keeping on" when all and everything seemed opposed to their forward movement. It is a spirituality expressed in song, in dance, in prayer, in preaching, and most important, in living each day as best they could in solidarity with one another and their God over against the principalities and powers of their time.

The story of African American spirituality is the story of the African American people, a people with deeply sunk African roots and strong, sturdy American branches. It is the story of the self-manifestation of a "wonderworking" God in their midst, providing them hope for the future and the courage to continue their struggle for a freedom both physical and spiritual over against those who would keep them bound and downtrodden.

In order to understand African American spirituality, it is necessary to tell the story of the African American people from their beginnings on the continent of Africa to the present day, surveying their journey through slavery in the past to a present mixed with blessings of wealth but also poverty, and a future filled with yet more challenges but also with the Holy Spirit of God.

In this work I attempt to present African American spirituality as it has emerged from its roots in the African traditional religions through its encounter with Christianity during slavery and as it was refined in antebellum slavery to its ongoing development up to the challenges of the twenty-first century. I seek to trace the evolution of African American (Black) spirituality from its roots in the peoples and cultures of West and Central Africa to the birthing of a liberating spirituality in the United States that gave strength and identity to an oppressed and marginalized people. This spirituality is a river that runs in flood and ebb in keeping with the situations of the people for whom it expresses life's hopes, fears, and relationships with their Creator God. It has many tributaries that flow across the United States, but its source is in the American South. It changes shapes, flows in every direction of the compass, changes hue and voice, but it speaks the truth of African American faith, a truth that cannot be dammed up or forced underground.

As part of this discussion I examine both Black Protestantism and Black Catholicism, how they relate and in what ways they differ, as well as womanist spirituality as a source of renewal for the Black community.

Chapter 1 explores the world of African traditional religions: African cosmology and philosophy, African music and dance, and spirit possession, laying the foundations for African spirituality. My emphasis is on the Western and Central parts of Africa, where the majority of those enslaved originated. Chapter 2 discusses the nascent religious world of the slaves: from the exportation of African worldviews and traditions (Africanisms) to the hush arbors and praise houses of the South, along with the slaves' initial encounter with Christianity and later with the religious fervor of the Great Awakenings.

Chapter 3 explores the response of the enslaved to Christianity in greater detail by discussing themes that emerge from and are prevalent in African American spirituality. Chapter 4 discusses the Negro spirituals, songs that voiced the spirituality and faith of enslaved Africans in the United States, exploring their development, hidden radical meanings, and viability to the present day. They are the forerunners of all Black music and of much American music.

Chapter 5 unfolds the emergence and development of the Black church and its influences on African American spirituality. It also explores the waning of some forms of African American spirituality and the emergence of new forms during the period between the end of the Civil War and the beginning of the civil rights movement. Chapter 6 discusses the spirituality that emerged from the civil rights and Black theology movements and explores different branches of these movements and their impact upon the Black community.

The role of women of African descent in the theology and spirituality of their community is still an unwritten document, although in the last twenty-five years emerging womanist theologians have begun to fill the gaps in our story with the voices of Black women. Therefore, in Chapter 7, I unfold the spirituality of Black women and how their steadfast faith in a God who saves enabled the Black community to survive. Finally, Chapter 8 discusses contemporary black spirituality as well as the challenges to it and how these can or may be overcome.

Chapter 8 also briefly discusses the reemergence of African religions, especially the Yoruba tradition, and the impact of Afro-Catholic-Latino/a religions on Black Christians in the United States today; a fuller discussion is beyond the scope of this book. Throughout, the text presents and discusses the spirituality of both African American Protestant and Catholic Christians. Because the emphasis in this work is presenting a general picture of African American Christian spirituality, it is impossible to include in-depth discussions of individual denominations or to go beyond mainstream Christian spirituality to include other religions of the African American community, which include Islam, Buddhism, and Judaism, among others.

This work would not have been possible without the steadfast support and patience of Robert Ellsberg of Orbis Books. Thank you. It is long overdue but is the fruit of many years of reading, writing, teaching, and lecturing on and about African American spirituality in various settings. The questions raised by students and workshop and conference participants have helped me formulate and shape the ideas herein and have inspired and continue to challenge me in many ways.

1

What Is Africa to Me?

African Roots

What is Africa to me:
Copper sun or scarlet sea . . .
One three centuries removed.
—Countee Cullen[1]

African Origins

More than 450 years have passed since the first Africans, initially Spanish speaking and probably Roman Catholic,[2] came to the Americas, but the question of the extent to which aspects of African culture were passed down to their descendants is still a matter of discussion and debate for many.

As Countee Cullen, a Harlem Renaissance poet, relates in his poem "Heritage," quoted in part above, by the twentieth century African heritage was regarded with both pride and disdain by most African Americans who, in company with all Americans, had been taught to regard the people of Africa as inferior, pagan savages who needed Christian conversion and Western civilization. For centuries this view has affected the way in which scholars not only looked at Africa and its people and how they wrote about Africa but also how they regarded African Americans. It has also affected the self-understanding and self-identity of African Americans. Fortunately, in the latter half of the twentieth century these

9

attitudes began to change as more scholars, especially those of African descent, embarked on significant research projects that tapped into sources and references hitherto ignored, overlooked, or misinterpreted.

Cullen clearly reveals this ambivalence as he dreams of a land he never knew: "Africa? A book one thumbs listlessly, till slumber comes" and had learned to be ashamed of:

> Quaint, outlandish heathen gods
> Black man fashioned out of rods . . .
> I belong to Jesus Christ, preacher of humility;
> Heathen gods are not for me.[3]

Yet, while asserting the superiority of his Christian faith, Cullen acknowledges its psychic cost and reveals his inner yearning for a connection between himself and the God he worships; a hunger for a god who understands him because that God himself has experienced the pain of being Black:

> Wishing he I served were black . . . ,
> Thinking then it would not lack
> precedent of pain to guide it.[4]

It is this inner yearning to understand themselves and their God that helped to form the spirituality of African Americans, a people who came into being as a result of forces much larger than themselves.

In this chapter I set forth the foundations of that spirituality, rooted in the African traditional religion of their forefathers and foremothers in Africa. For Africans and African Americans "share a common racial heritage, a common relationship to the dominant Western culture, and a common spirit. This common spirit found in people of African descent is an attitude that sees all of life in the context of the encounter with the Divine, and the all-embracing vision of the Divine-human encounter—which is merely the essential clue to understanding the nature of Black spirituality—and is rooted in a distinctive and ancient worldview."[5]

Who were these ancestors? What did they believe and why? How did they express themselves religiously? What was their contribution to the survival and formation of those who now name themselves both African and American?

African Religious Systems

First, it must be acknowledged that the use of words such as *religion* and *Africa* are somewhat artificial, as they are Western constructions that have forced the religious systems of the people of "Africa" (a continent made up of many nations and peoples) into a structure not of their own design. Africa itself, obviously, is not one people with one cosmological worldview, one culture, one language, or one history. Thus, there is not one spiritual or religious understanding or one word that encapsulates the totality of their worldview. Religion, as such, is not studied or analyzed; it is lived, for "to live is to be religious; to be religious is to greet God with many names in the multiple circumstances of one's life here and now."[6]

It took the Atlantic slave trade and the colonialism that fed and shaped it to impose a cultural uniformity on the varying religious traditions of Africans. This effort toward uniformity came into existence in the late 1700s, around the same time as the sociopolitical notion of race based on skin color. Such a perception ignored the richness of the language, cultures, and ethnic identities that defined African life.[7]

This perception also affects how we look at African traditional religion. Strictly speaking, *traditional religion* cannot be described from an African point of view because that point of view, as noted above, does not include *religion* in the Western sense of the word. Our descriptions of these beliefs and practices are "inherently Western"[8] and" based on the unconscious (and at times conscious) desire to make Christianity seem superior and African religions primitive." They are also affected "by African Christian interpretations, which strive "to make African religions more 'normal' by making them look more Christian or Western."[9]

Admittedly, however, a form of unity does exist in the midst of the diversity, one that defines a larger shared culture, philosophy, and even religious perspective. It is this unity that I will be discussing in order to present a limited overview of the cosmological systems that African peoples share and that were "carried in the memories of enslaved Africans across the Atlantic."[10] While recognizing the harsh and repressive impact of capture, imprisonment, and enslavement on the Africans brought to the Americas, much of their worldview was retained.

Jacob Olupona confirms this, noting:

> In the beginning, [there] was a deep religious and spiritual heritage vouchsafed in myths, rituals, and symbols. But as a result of Africa's contact with the outside world, especially under very ignominious circumstances—exploration, slave trade, and colonialism—significant aspects of the traditions were lost or modified to conform to the taste of the conquerors and the new rulers. A central event in the African's encounter with colonialism was the former's conversion to Islam and Christianity and their imbibing of new religious traditions from the Middle East and Europe. Africans responded to this encounter with resistance and fierceness and in most cases adapted the new spirituality by domesticating the new traditions and making them truly African. . . . A similar domesticating process affected African religions that were transported to the New World mainly by Africans who left against their own will as slaves to labor on the plantations. . . . There, in their new environment, the slaves adapted their master's religion but still kept

on praying to their African deities and dancing to their music in the new land.[11]

African Traditional Religion

As already stated, African traditional religion cannot be fully discussed using Western theological perspectives such as monotheism, polytheism, or pantheism, as these terms too often err through oversimplification of the rich diversity of the African religious experience. Monotheism and polytheism, for example, are not seen as opposites or contradictory by most Africans but as complementary expressions of faith. This is because of the almost universal belief in a Supreme Being, transcendent yet open to the needs of the people, and lesser entities that are seen as intermediaries between the Supreme God and the people. It is these lesser deities, which also include the ancestors, who serve as the immanent manifestation of God. Benjamin Ray describes this understanding as follows:

> Having formed the immutable structures of sky and earth in the orderly human cycle of birth, life, and death, the Supreme Creator God remains in the background like a distant ruler or patriarch, occasionally intervening but generally leaving the fortunes and misfortunes of everyday life to lesser agents, the gods and spirits. Both kinds of divinity, the One Creator God and the many lesser powers, are essential to the full range of traditional religious experience.[12]

Basically, African traditional religion is the "indigenous religion of Africans. It is that religion which emerged from the sustaining faith held by the forbears of the present generation of Africans. . . . It is a religion whose founders cannot be traced, no matter how far we went back into history."[13] As A. E. Orobator affirms:

African ways of speaking about God show us that Africans live in a religiously charged, even supercharged, environment. The African religious universe is populated by numerous gods, goddesses, divinities, deities, spirit beings, and ancestors. But this does not obscure the belief in One Supreme Being, whose eternal will holds sway over the destiny of all creation. . . . Belief in this God has strong moral implications for human beings in their daily existence, both individually and communally.[14]

One of the simplest ways to understand what Africans believe is to listen to the proverbs and songs about God and the names they use for God. Many of the proverbs are still used today in the United States by African Americans. They relate to God's action in the world and how human beings interact with God. For example,

- God is never in a hurry, but is always there at the right time (Ethiopia);
- If God dishes you rice in a basket, do not wish to eat soup (Sierra Leone);
- We do not see God; we see only the works of God (Ethiopia).[15]

The names of God are plentiful as well. Each makes a theological statement about God because they "tell of God's nature and attribute particular qualities and functions to God." In so doing, they reveal how God relates to humanity. They name God as shield (Osarugue) and refuge (Igbinose); as merciful (Ngonidzashe) and all powerful (Osasere), among many others. Many are given names that reflect a positive characteristic of God such as child of God (Karuhanga) and will of God (Kudakwashe).[16]

These names and proverbs reveal the all-encompassing nature of God for African people. They recognize that God is active in all that they do, and they continually experience

God's loving and affirming guidance. This theological worldview is expressed in a "complex of ideas, feelings, and rites" that are based on a common set of beliefs, including a belief in two worlds, visible and invisible, both of which involve community and hierarchy; a belief in the intersection of these two worlds, the transcendent not contradicting the immanent; and a belief in a Supreme Deity, Creator and Father of all that exists.[17]

Yet another way to look at African traditional religion is by pulling together several general themes that appear in all of its expressions. As we shall see, many of these themes persist in the Christianity adapted by African slaves that eventually developed into Black Christianity in its myriad forms.

The most common belief for all Africans is "belief in one Supreme God who has many names: Oludumare among the Yoruba, Nkulunkulu among the Zulu, and Amma among the Dogon. This God can be male or female, father or mother depending on the society while in some, such as the Dogon, Amma has both male and female characteristics."[18] God is seen as both immanent and transcendent, near to those who seek yet distant enough that those who believe must actively search.[19] Because of God's transcendence, Africans are engaged on a daily basis with divinities who act as intermediaries and intercessors between them and God. At the risk of imposing Western Christian understandings, these intermediaries can be seen as similar to the angels and saints of the Catholic faith or another belief system because they include persons who once lived and now after death are venerated as ancestors as well as those long dead whose names have been passed down from generation to generation.

Ancestor veneration is not worship. Only the high God is worshiped. Venerating the ancestors and asking for their help in overcoming illness or grief or danger are critical and integral aspects of African traditional religion. The ancestors are venerated because they serve as "a source and symbol of lineage; as models of ethical life, service, and social achievement to the community; and because they are spiritual intercessors between humans and the Creator."[20] As Maulana Karenga affirms, "Ancient African religions stress the necessary balance between one's collective identity and responsibility as a member of society and one's personal identity and responsibility. Like religion itself, a person is defined as an integral part of a definite community, to which she/he belongs and in which she/he finds identity and relevance."[21] Thus, as John Mbiti affirms, "I am because we are, and since we are, therefore I am."[22]

A second common factor is the profound respect Africans have for nature. Because they believe that all things live in a religious universe, everything in that universe therefore has religious relevance.[23] An "unbreakable bond" exists among humans, the divine, and nature itself, and it is reciprocal.

Finally, death and immortality are of critical importance. Death is a stage in human development, one reflective of cosmic patterns, yet not an end in itself for it is also a "transition in life to personal and collective immortality."[24] Personal immortality occurs through one's children, relatives, rites of remembrance, and one's significant body of work or actions. Collective memory comes through one's people and the community's ongoing memory of a person. The dead continue to live in the hearts, minds, and acts of their family and community and thus become ancestors to be honored and called upon in times of need.[25]

Life in/as Community

How do these themes in African traditional religion come together in actual life? First, it is recognized that there is a vital relationship between the life of the individual and that of his or her community. Individualism, especially as it has developed in Western society, is unthinkable, because an African is defined by his or her community and the roles that community sets before him or her. There is a "vital union," a bond that brings together all beings living and dead. "That union is the life-giving principle in all," and is the result of communion.[26] All of life is participatory life. An individual participates within his or her community and within the sacred life of his or her ancestors while at the same time preparing for his or her own continuance through offspring and/or other means. As a result, all of life is sacred and indivisible, winding in a continuous cycle from birth through childhood and into adulthood and on to death, a death that is, however, a beginning rather than an end for it is in constant communication with the world of the living. Thus, according to Congolese theologian Vincent Mulago, all of life can be understood as community in blood, the principal and primordial element, and as community in possessions, a concomitant element making life possible. He affirms that Africans have meaningful existence in their own eyes and in the eyes of society only to the extent that they participate in life and transmit life.[27] The "we" of community serves as the foundation for the "I" of a person's life.

Second, one's being can be enhanced or diminished through what is seen as "vital power" or *ntu*. When a person is elevated to a new position or role in the community such as being named a king or queen, shaman, or chief, an ontic change takes place, one that leads to a profound transformation resulting in a new form of being that causes a person to act in a manner and style that befits the new situation or status.[28]

Similarly, a person's being can be diminished by evil or injustice, which blocks the flow of vital power, leaving him or her disconnected from God, the ancestors, and descendants, separate from all that makes life possible.[29]

Sin

The African understanding of sin, as a result, must be understood within the greater context of communal life, which itself is a much wider concept than it is in Western thought. For African people, life "embraces the world of the yet-to-be-born, the living, the living dead (ancestors), and all other categories of animal and plant life as well as the world of nature.[30] Life is the most basic category of the African's religious worldview. Sin is therefore understood as "anything that diminishes, opposes or destroys life." As life is a shared category, sin is an attack or disruption of community as a whole, not just on the individual. As Orobator confirms:

> Sin is not a reality to be dealt with solely on the level of abstraction; it manifests itself as concrete and experiential and has palpable effects on the destiny of the individual in community. There is always an agent (human or spiritual) behind or at the origin of the evil or sinful act, and this act exists as such only in the actions of people toward one another. Sin is relational. Something is considered as sinful insofar as it destroys the life of the doer and the life that he or she shares with the rest of the community and nature.[31]

The criterion for good and evil in the African world is humanity itself. Theirs is an anthropocentric perspective, one that ascribes good and evil to several sources. For example, the Bantu people of Central Africa see the world as *ntu*, a vital force or power that flows throughout and within all of creation. They believe that "actions thought favorable to the blossoming of life, capable of conserving and protecting life, of making it flower and increasing the vital potentiality of the community are, for these reasons, considered good" but those acts "thought prejudicial to the life of the individual or of the community are judged evil."[32] This is because human life is the most valuable good for the Bantu people. The ideal is not only to live to a good old age protected from anxieties but more importantly to remain, even after death, a vital force continually reinforced and vivified in and through one's children and their children. This *muntu* ideal reveals that every human act is judged by its relationship to life and the afterlife.[33]

Clearly, life for African people is one in constant communication with the divine. There is no division between the sacred and secular worlds; both interact continuously in ways that are life enhancing. The African worldview is not abstract or objective but subjective and holistic; it is the vital core of all life, connecting humanity to the Supreme Being, the lesser intermediaries, all created life, and the earth itself. As Orobator explains:

> Religion permeates the whole life of the black African—their personal, family, and sociopolitical life. Religion has the psychological social function of integration and equilibrium. It enables people to understand and value themselves, to achieve integration, accept their situation in life, to control their anguish. Thanks to religion, the duality between human beings and their world, visible and invisible, is overcome and unification achieved.[34]

Put another way, Orobator affirms the deep religiosity of African peoples:

> Africans are a very deeply religious people. . . . The awareness of the divine is so strong that you can see, hear, feel, and touch it in the way people talk, behave, even worship, sing, and dance. . . . The African universe is charged with a palpable spiritual energy; this energy comes from faith in the existence of many spiritual realities: gods, goddesses, deities, ancestral spirits, and so on. African spirituality draws on the energy that comes from this awareness that the human being is not alone in the universe; the universe delineates a shared space between creatures and their creator.[35]

African Spirituality

Jacob Olupona defines the African spiritual experience as "one in which the 'divine' or the 'sacred' realm interpenetrates into the daily experience of the human person so much that religion, culture, and society are imperatively interrelated."[36]

Having laid the foundation for African spirituality in an articulation of African traditional religion, it is now possible to present an overview of the spirituality that flows from this religious perspective. It is a holistic spirituality in which the Divine is not separated from but intertwined with the daily life of human beings, resulting in an ongoing relationship between them and God before birth, throughout life, and continuing after death. African spirituality can be seen as the expression of one's experience of God as experienced in communion with others, an encounter that is ongoing and ever present. As a result, the African religious worldview is by definition a spiritual worldview for it is through life with its rituals, its taboos, its holy days, its priests and priestesses, that the life of the community is ordered and regulated, and it is through symbol—song, dance, spoken word, vestments, holy objects—that humanity's relationship with the Supreme Being is experienced and expressed.

Creation Stories

A major component of this worldview is the role played by myths of origin or creation stories. Ethnographer Dominique Zahan affirms their importance in African spirituality:

One can say that in the African spiritual worldview, myths about the origin of the world, of death, of various institutions are thought to be the key to understanding traditional life. From these myths information is derived about the nature, characteristics, and function of the deities. These myths, which differ from one ethnic group to another, yield images of the different supernatural entities. The first, of course, is the Supreme Being, who remains supreme but like Juno or Jupiter is not beyond being influenced.[37]

African creation myths, like all such myths or stories, are a means of explaining the origins of human life as well as the human social order. They provide us with descriptions of "the social and cultural building blocks of African societies" and by so doing "give meaning to life cycle events and the moral rules of everyday life."[38] They provide a connection to the past and serve as guides to the future for Africans.

African understandings of creation, the origins of the world and its inhabitants, are based on a "time frame best described as 'before time,'" which is "primordial time; no one in living memory recalls that time, but all carry a collective memory of the events that make up that time of 'before before.'"[39] Again stories, songs, proverbs, and so on are the means through which these memories are shared and handed down.

Orobator provides an excellent introduction to many of these stories in his *Theology Brewed in an African Pot*. Here, I highlight some significant aspects of these stories or myths. All reveal God as Creator of all things, living and nonliving, and most also have an explanation for why things are the way they are, for example, how the ancestors came into being and their purpose as mediators. The stories establish the world's beings and their interactions, showing how strife, jealousy, and anger entered the world often because of the faults or failings of humankind, who disobey God's laws. One such story is that of the people now living in modern-day Tanzania:

> Kiumbi, the creator, created the ancestors and all things that they required. These ancestors became mediators between God the creator and the living members of society. Kiumbi had his dwelling place in the sky. Formerly Kiumbi had regular commerce with people. But the people disobeyed him, eating eggs that he had ordered them not to eat. They did this because they were cheated by a person whose name was Kiriamagi. As a result, God withdrew himself to a distant abode. Now the people were alone, without fellowship with God. But he sometimes visited them. People attempted

to build a tower to reach God's place and thereby attain the former fellowship with him. But the higher they built, the farther God's place receded. . . . Eventually, God punished the people with a severe famine, during which all the people died except two youths, a boy and a girl. All the people on earth descend from this pair. Since then, man's fellowship with God has been remote and communication with him has to be sought with the ancestors who are closer to him than the living members of the society (Asu, Pare/Tanzania).[40]

These and other creation stories attribute creation to a divine being who either creates or delegates "the power to create" to others. Creation is not limited or finite but a cosmic affair and God (Divinity) alone is the source and explanation for all that exists. Creation can take place in various ways, simply by calling forth different elements of nature, by organizing nature's chaos, or by using various materials or other entities. To create means to give life and all of nature is imbued with life: humans, plants, animals, and all objects of nature. This is the source of Africans' respect for all of creation and leads to the requirement of harmony with nature, a critical aspect of human life. Some aspects of nature are sacred and/or revered and are not to be eaten or are to be used only for medicinal or curative purposes so as to retain and/or preserve harmony. They are an often important part of sacred rituals performed throughout the lives of African peoples.[41]

Sacred Ritual

A second critical factor in African spirituality is the role that ritual, especially as accompanied by song and dance, plays in daily life. It is in ritual that "the relationship between the human being and the divine being is expressed and achieved."[42] Rituals are acts of invoking and communicating with God and God's intermediaries, especially the ancestors. Ritual is a form of worship that usually involves, as all worship does for Africans, singing, dancing, and music in all of its forms. The aim of most rituals is to help the people with their problems and/or to make sense of the interaction between the spiritual and material worlds and to bring harmony. Ritual is at the very heart of African society because it creates "a different world of symbols, a world that re-creates and recombines culture in a progressive way." Rituals, especially individual rites serve as road maps pointing the way to a deeper understanding of the social and cosmic orders, of which the spiritual is a part.[43]

Thus, dance, ritual, and ceremony are critical aspects of African life. They provide the "dramatic elements" of the religious traditions.[44] If, as Mbiti asserts, religion is life and life therefore is religion for Africans, it must also be affirmed that life is communal and kinship plays a critical role, especially family and clan. Fisher acknowledges that "in the context of the social structure, dance, rhythm, drumming, song, and mime all express a way of thinking, of feeling, and of communicating with one another."[45] Africans are and historically were an oral people. Words, therefore, have power and significance to them but also require other elements to, as it were, enflesh them, such as mime and dance. As Fisher affirms, "The cultural language is as important as the spoken tongue [for it] creates community; it enhances life; it establishes a religious sense of the presence of the spiritual order and moral values. It creates the environment for connecting the past with the future and change."[46]

African rituals are performed for many different reasons and purposes depending on the needs of individuals and the larger community. They serve "to cure illnesses, initiate the young, diagnose problems, and restore social harmony."[47] They also explain the causes of human misfortune and open the participants to spiritual blessings. Rituals "express moral values, reinforce social unity, and provide psychological therapy" for all engaged in them.[48]

One very important rite is the rite of passage, the coming of age of young men and women. Ray discusses their importance and significance as follows:

> They sustain the social order by creating new social and moral bonds between people in order to continue the established social order. Rites of passage create meaningful transformations in the human life cycle (birth, puberty, marriage, death), in the seasonal and agricultural cycle, and in the installation of persons to high office. These transformations are done according to a threefold ritual process consisting of rites of separation, of transition, and of reincorporation. For example, children are taken away from their families, transformed into young adults through ritual markings and instruction, and returned to society with a new status and social responsibilities.[49]

Song and dance are a part of every feast and festival, of every ritual, for they bring the people together and enable them to immerse themselves in the holy, the cosmos that surrounds them. Fisher discusses the significance of dance in depth, noting that

> African dance is unique in its celebration of events in life from the significant to the ordinary. The African dances when a baby is born and named and at puberty rites; the African dances in rejoicing at marriages and mourning at funerals. The African dances at festivals, when the yams are harvested, to thank the spiritual powers for food and life. . . . To get a job done, they sing while they work in the fields, calling and shouting to one another, while moving in rhythm to the beating of drums or tools. The result is to create solidarity and harmony.[50]

Africans interact with the spirit world in a number of ways, including through dance, prayers, and invocations. Music usually is a vital part of any religious ceremony and dance as well. Religious dances are also social as "their purpose is to generate systemic control over all forces of good or evil for the harmony between the spirit and material worlds, and as social control over the behavior of the people by means of oracles, shrines, and customs."[51]

As we shall see, song and dance are critical aspects of African spirituality that were carried over the waters to the Americas with enslaved Africans, providing a connection with their past and a path leading to their future. Rituals such as the ring shout and the conversion experience carried with them overtones and underlayings from their African ancestry and helped those enslaved to make sense of the new and contrary worlds in which they found themselves unwilling captives.

Human Agencies

A third component of African spirituality consists of "human agencies, religious functionaries, and those who have undergone apprenticeship in ritual technique such as priests attached to specific shrines, diviners, and more informally herbalists" as well as sacred kings and queens and chiefs seen as sacred intermediaries between the people and the divinities.[52] These agencies serve to enhance or sometimes block the vital force necessary to maintain life. They preside over the rites and rituals, guide the community in observing and performing them, and serve as critical links for the community to divinity.

The ancestors play a significant role in human agency. As previously discussed, they are former living persons who, having lived honorable lives, are venerated after their death. The ancestors are integral to the African cosmology because they serve as the connection between the living and the dead in the cycle of life, death, and rebirth. They serve as intermediaries for their living relatives, as guides and often as goads to living a good life. Because life is seen as "a cycle that moves from birth to death and, passing through the spiritual/ancestor world, comes back to reincarnated birth." Africans see death as only a transition from the human plane to the spiritual/ancestor world.[53]

There are five essential traits of African ancestorship:

- An ancestor maintains some binding blood ties with the living members of his or her family, clan or community.
- The experience of death offers the ancestor a privileged place of closeness to God.
- He or she is able to mediate or intercede on behalf of the living family or clan members.
- He or she [as a mediator] is entitled to mandatory and regular communication and consultation (invocation, libation, ritual offerings, sacrifices, etc.) with the living.
- To become an ancestor [the living dead], a person must have distinguished himself or herself in service and led an exemplary life in community.[54]

African spirituality is a spirituality of "stewardship, renewal and affirmation of faith in the integrity of creation as a gift and the shared patrimony of all humanity." As such, it is also a "spirituality of balance, harmony, and wholeness, sustained by an active faith in creation as God's gift."[55] It is a song and dance to celebrate the birth of a child and the child's naming; a cry of loving anguish from the hearts of those who mourn a death while rejoicing in that person's ascendancy to the ancestors; it is a whoop, a holler, an exultation in times of celebration and a weeping moan in times of pain. It is the very soul of African people.

Out from Africa

The African people who were brought, most against their will, to the Americas carried within them the African cosmological worldview discussed in this chapter. Finding themselves strangers and aliens in a foreign land, often without their priests, priestesses, and diviners, they were still able to retain sufficient knowledge and understanding of their religious foundations to be able to maintain many of their beliefs, more or less intact, for generations. Those Africans who found themselves on Catholic plantations, especially in the Caribbean and South America, were introduced to Christianity from the very beginning of their enslavement. Finding much in Catholicism to suit them, they, in most instances, simply layered the Christian faith onto already existing beliefs, seeing no conflict in doing so. At the same time many African Catholics, especially in the Carolinas and Louisiana, came to the American colonies/states with prior knowledge of and experience of Catholicism, especially those from Kongo (today's Angola), the first West African nation voluntarily to convert to Roman Catholicism (1491) and to establish independent relations with the Vatican State.

On Protestant plantations, however, conversion to Christianity was not initially welcomed or encouraged due to the owners' fears that the newly baptized slaves would have to be freed. This persisted until the early to mid 1800s when the Baptists and Methodists began to make inroads into Anglican piety. The delay, however, allowed the slaves to retain and pass on African understandings and habits, often for generations. After the Great Awakenings of the eighteenth (1730s–40s) and nineteenth (1800–1830) centuries, however, it became much more difficult to maintain continuity with their African past as all evidence of such connections was strongly condemned and punished. This was especially true after 1807, when the external slave trade ended in the United States and most slaves were "homegrown." As shall be seen in later chapters, however, the slaves still managed to hold on to much that was African in origin in their religiosity. Their faith, whether Catholic or Protestant, played a significant role in their planning and carrying out of slave rebellions, which will be discussed in Chapter 3.

African indigenous traditional spirituality persists to this day. It can be distinguished from African American spirituality in a number of ways, as we shall see herein. First, the former includes no understanding or notion of original sin or redemption, a fact which caused significant problems for slave masters seeking to instill the "fear of God" in their slaves. Thus, there is no final judgment either. The religious experience of Africans can be seen as a product of a cyclical, repetitive time, one lacking the "mark of eternity," as opposed to Christianity's linear time scale. For Africans, the past and future are always connected, and time is unending. As a result, salvation "becomes a repetitive undertaking of which the protagonist is the individual."[56] Believers themselves are not dependent solely on a transcendent being for their redemption, but also on themselves and their actions and failures as part of a living community. This understanding reveals the critical significance of human as well as divine action and intervention, an understanding that was clearly carried over in the religious and spiritual lives of those Africans who overtime were transformed into African Americans.

As shall be seen in Chapter 2, the slaves slowly began to mesh, some willingly, others under duress, the worldview of their ancestors and their former lives with those of Christianity, both Protestant and Catholic. Taking place over decades and centuries, from this feat of inculturation came a rechristianizing of European Christianity, a Black Christianity that was grounded in the pursuit of freedom for its proponents and the recognition of their humanity as creations of God. This Christianity persists today in the twenty-first century and has had a profound and lasting impact not only on Americans of African descent but on all Americans in all aspects of culture, particularly in terms of music, language, and spirituality.

2

Lord, How Come Me Here?

Building Community

The "spirituality" of a people refers to the animating and integrative power that constitutes the principal frame of meaning for individual and collective experiences. . . . African spirituality is never disembodied but always integrally connected with the dynamic movement of life. . . . Unity in diversity is another metaphor for African spirituality.

—Peter J. Paris[1]

Unity in Diversity

This "unity in diversity" is clearly revealed in the spirituality of people of African descent in the United States. Over the centuries of America's Peculiar Institution, as slavery was called, more than ten million African men, women, and children were stolen from African villages and trading posts, loaded on ships, and dispersed throughout the Americas and the Caribbean. Seen as unworthy of the dignity and respect normally accorded to human beings because of their skin color,[2] they were shackled and whipped, beaten and raped, and transported thousands of miles from their homes, families, and communities. They were brought, loose packed or tight packed, along with elephant tusks and other cargo, in the holds of ships named after Jesus and his mother to the islands of the Caribbean and the shores of North and South America, fated to spend the rest of their lives as human cattle, slaves with no rights a white person need observe.[3] Although they came from many tribes and traditions, they were able to forge a unity that helped them preserve their sanity during the Middle Passage and their lives and spirits for the centuries that slavery endured in the Americas.

Despite the horrors of the Middle Passage, the loss of life, family, and tribe, as well as the denial of their humanity, these African men and women were able to connect with one another, including those who had once been their enemies, because of their shared plight. Connections were first constructed in the camps and pens in which they were held on the African coasts while waiting for the slave ships to arrive. Confinement below decks, especially for the men, forced them to interact with one another and share languages so that they could plot rebellion on board. It is believed there were more than 250 shipboard rebellions, most, sadly, unsuccessful.[4] They were still able to sing as their ancestors had done and use the music as a means of communication as well. Music—song, dance, praise—was a critical aspect of their lives as it enabled them to withstand the traumatic conditions in which they lived. They sang of their fears and their sorrows but they also sang of their hopes and dreams. They sang of their faith in Someone greater than themselves, and in so doing they sang a new people into life.

Their quest was to understand their present in light of their past. This is the significance of *sankofa*,[5] to remember whence you came in order to understand where you are now and where you are going in the future. They sought clarity about their new and horrific situation asking, usually in song or in fervent prayer, "Lord, how come me here? I wish I'd never been born." Yet this seemingly negative perspective was countered by a persistent hope in a freedom soon to come as they slowly coalesced into a community of faith. So they also sang: "I'm so glad trouble don't last always."

Who were these people, enslaved yet capable of singing of a faith that could overcome all with which life had assaulted them? What enabled these African slaves to persevere in the face of the chaos into which they had been thrown? How did they manage to create life in the face of the constant threat of death? They were able to do so because of their recognition of a higher power than themselves who could and would right all wrongs, banish all sorrows, chastise the wicked, and release those in captivity. The spirituality of African Americans, grounded in their African ancestry despite efforts to cut those ties, is not just a spirituality of action; it is a spirituality of resilience and resistance. In the words of theologian Kelly Brown Douglas:

> Historically, a *spirituality of resistance* has been central to black people's survival and wholeness in a society that demeans their very black humanity. Such spirituality is characterized by a sense of connection to one's own heritage as well as to the divine. As such, it provides black men and women with a buffer of defense against white cultural characterizations of them as beings unworthy of freedom, dignity, even life. At the same time, a spirituality of resistance grants them, especially black women, a sense of control over their own bodies.[6]

This liberating spirituality enabled them not only to survive centuries of slavery but to come together as a community of faith that would not accept defeat or diminishment at the hands of others inimical to their very existence. It is a spirituality that persists to the present day despite the new challenges and obstacles confronting persons of African descent in the United States.

Africanisms in the United States

The ties between African peoples and those brought to the "New World" were never completely severed. Rather, threads of African life and culture persisted in the language, rituals, music, dance, preaching, stories, and prayers of the slaves. Brought to the Americas predominantly from West and Central Africa, they may have had different languages, myths, and rituals, but their underlying religious worldview was basically the same. As Albert Raboteau notes, "Worship of the gods, veneration of the ancestors, African-style drumming and dancing, rites of initiation, priests and priestesses, spirit possession, ritual sacrifice, sacred emblems and taboos, extended funerals, and systems of divination and magic all attest to the living African heritage of Black people."[7] So the African gods did not die in America but were transformed in ways about which we are still learning.

The question for discussion here, however, is how much of this worldview was retained and passed on in the colonies that made up the United States? Although few continue to assert that all knowledge and memory of the African past was totally destroyed for the American slaves by the horrors of the Middle Passage or of slavery itself, the extent of those memories retained is still being debated. Albert Raboteau indicates the two conflicting arguments historically proposed. The first is "that African retentions in the United States were negligible because the African was almost totally stripped of his culture by the process of enslavement." The other asserts that the system of slavery "did not destroy the slaves' African culture and a considerable number of Africanisms not only were retained and passed on but continue to define Afro-American culture in the United States."[8]

Most historians of both the African past and the African American present, however, support the second argument and especially find accord in acknowledging the critical role that religion (African traditional religions, Christianity, and Islam) has played in perpetuating Africanisms. Joseph Holloway, a professor of Pan African studies, defines Africanisms as "those elements of culture found in the new world that are traceable to an African origin."[9] Historically, even those who supported the argument for them tended to lump all attributes of the slaves' past to one general location—Sub-Saharan Africa or West Africa. However, it is today recognized that certain parts and peoples of Africa were of greater significance than others in the formation of African American culture and traditions. Holloway explains that "Although West African slaves arrived in greater numbers, the Bantu of Central Africa possessed the largest homogeneous culture among the imported Africans and, consequently, had the strongest impact on the future development of African American culture and language."[10]

The majority of African Americans do not know from which particular people or part of Western or Central Africa their ancestors may have come. Yet, as a result of studies of those enslaved in particular regions of the South, it is clear that the slave owners were often quite selective, choosing particular peoples based on the type of work they were to do in order to avoid losses due to illness or having to train hands for unfamiliar work. "As Southern Planters became more keenly aware of the agricultural practices in Africa, they used their newly acquired knowledge as a basis for selecting Africans for importation to North America. Thus African occupational designations in the New World were largely determined by African culture, ethnicity, and regions of origin."[11]

Because the field hands were relatively free from exposure to Western culture, it is this group that had the greatest influence on African American culture and traditions. Artisans and domestic servants, in contrast, usually had a closer working relationship with European Americans and, as a result, often found their cultural identities compromised by the master's efforts to control and "civilize" them. Holloway believes that

> given the restraints imposed on artisans and domestic servants by plantation owners, one may logically conclude that the cultures of the Congo-Angola region of

Central Africa rather than those of West Africa were dominant in North America. West African culture nevertheless supplied mainstream southern society with Africanisms through a process of reciprocal acculturation between Africans and European Americans.[12]

This influence is especially seen in the southern states of the Carolinas and Georgia where field slaves came mainly from Central Africa and shared a common heritage, tradition, religious worldview, and language, and most specifically in the Gullah peoples who lived in relative isolation on the Sea Islands off the coasts of these states. They spoke (and still speak) an English-based Creole language that contains many African words and even retains much African grammatical and sentence structure. Their retentions can be found in their storytelling, folk beliefs, crafts, and farming and fishing habits, all of which show strong influences from West and Central Africa. They were selected and brought from rice-farming areas in Africa to introduce rice farming in the southern colonies.[13] It is known today that many of their ancestors were brought from what is now the African nation of Sierra Leone.

In *The Gullah People and Their African Heritage*, William Pollitzer and David Moltko-Hansen describe these retentions of African practices:

Once the Bantu reached America they were able to retain much of their cultural identity. Enforced isolation of these Africans by plantation owners allowed them to retain their religion, philosophy, culture, folklore, folkways, folk beliefs, folktales, storytelling, naming practices, home economics, arts, kinship, and music. These Africanisms were shared and adopted by the various African ethnic groups of the field slave community, and they gradually developed into African-American cooking (soul food), music (jazz, blues, spirituals, Gospels), language, religion, philosophy, customs, and arts.[14]

Roman Catholic Influences

The first Africans in the United States, however, came with the Spanish Conquistadors and spoke little or no English. The date of 1619, usually given as when the first Africans arrived, applies only to the English colonies and English American history. The great majority of Africans who came in the sixteenth century were Ladinos, baptized Spanish-speaking Roman Catholics who either had been born in Latin America or lived in Spain. In the early 1500s Spain exiled hundreds of Black Ladinos. They came, some free but many enslaved, to the Americas, and became a critical source of labor and helped in establishing and maintaining the colonies. One of the earliest of these colonies, Deepwater Port, was founded around 1526 on St. Helen's Island off the South Carolina coast. It became the capital of colonial Florida and changed hands between the Spanish and the French repeatedly until after the American Revolution, when it was taken over by the English. One of the first to explore the Southwest was the Ladino Estevanico, and others helped to establish the cities of St. Augustine, Florida, and Los Angeles, California, in which they played critical roles politically, religiously, and socially.[15] As Cyprian Davis notes, "The baptismal registers, which began with the colony [of St. Augustine] and are the oldest ecclesiastical documents in American history, witness to the presence of Blacks and whites in this Spanish colonial town.[16]

It is in these Catholic Christians that some of the most significant African retentions can be seen. Catholicism, a Christian faith rich in symbol and ritual, spoke directly to the African soul, enabling much syncretization to take place. Catholic saints were meshed with African lesser deities and the ancestors, and Catholic rituals were incorporated into African rites, and vice versa. The clearest examples of this today are in the Caribbean islands and Brazil, which gave birth to new Afro-Catholic religions such as Candomblé, Santería, and Vodoun. In the United States, where the numbers of

Catholic slaves were fewer and therefore more susceptible to control, evidence of syncretism can still be found, especially in Louisiana, which gave birth to a unique group distinct from slaves and free Blacks. They were the "free persons of color" or Creoles who, though of African ancestry, were also of Spanish and French descent. Those enslaved in Louisiana were also able to retain much of their African culture because on Sundays, a day off for the slaves, they were permitted greater freedom to assemble and interact. After attending mass on Sundays they often went to Congo Square just north of Rampart Street and the French Quarter, where they danced in traditional ways, often dividing by tribal groups, and visited with one another.

Many Africans found Catholicism conducive to expressing their beliefs because of similarities in beliefs, structure, and rituals. Clarence Rivers has commented:

> The use of sacramentals (blessed objects), such as statues, pictures, candles, incense, holy water, rosaries, vestments, and relics, in Catholic ritual was more akin to the spirit of African piety than the sparseness of Puritan America, which held such objects to be idolatrous. Holy days, processions, Saints' feasts, days of fast and abstinence were all recognizable to the African who had observed the sacred days, festivals, and food taboos of his gods.[17]

Theologian Jamie Phelps affirms this as well, noting:

> One may argue that some points of African belief could have provided a basis for religious dialogue between African religions and Western Christianity. African belief in a supreme, all-powerful, omniscient, and immutable God is suggestive of the Christian understanding of the one true God.
>
> Some aspects of the African ancestor traditions seem to correlate with the Christian doctrine of the "communion of saints" in which the living and the dead

maintain a spiritual unity before the Lord, and what Catholic Christian worship has traditionally called the "Sacrifice of the Mass" was seen not only as a community celebration of God's presence in our lives but also as an actual re-enactment and memorial of the sacrifice of Jesus, who, in our place, died for our sins and to redeem us. . . . Even the concept of a spirit taking possession of an individual is not totally foreign to Christian concepts of the divine indwelling and the strengthening of one's faith by the celebration of the Sacraments.[18]

A critically important group were the Kongo people (present-day Angola), who took great pride in their Catholicism and persisted in its practice in the Americas. Theirs was a Christian country with "a fairly extensive system of schools and churches in addition to a high degree of literacy. The Kongolese were proud of their Christian and Catholic heritage, which they believed made them a distinctive people."[19]

However, for most Catholics, their introduction to Christianity was quite superficial as baptisms were done en masse, often as they were herded on board ships on the African coasts. Catechisms, when used, basically taught submission and obedience rather than the true doctrines or traditions of the church. The sacraments, especially that of marriage, were either denied them or ignored in response to economic demands. But, as shall be seen, many Catholics were eventually caught up in the spirit of the Great Awakenings (First, 1730s–40s; Second, 1800–1830), which encouraged a more personal and fervent experience of and relationship with Jesus the Christ.

Protestant Influences

In Protestant Christianity, although there was less opportunity for syncretism, there was a greater openness to the emotional expressiveness of the African people as they worshiped God, especially by the newly emerging Methodists and Baptists. More important, however, was the fact that, unlike in Catholic colonies where the slaves were immediately baptized, albeit poorly catechized, little effort was made to convert the slaves on Protestant plantations until the nineteenth century. This enabled the memories of African heritage to be retained and passed on to later generations for some time. This is especially true of the lowland plantations of the Carolinas and the Sea Islands off the Carolina and Georgia coasts, where isolation from white culture enabled the slaves to retain many forms of Africanisms. It is here, as well as in Catholic Louisiana, that the greatest number of Africanisms are to be found.

This does not mean that those enslaved in other parts of the United States lost all knowledge of their past. Rather, because of their smaller numbers, their occupations as artisans and house servants, and their greater contact with Africans of different cultures and traditions, their perspectives were also transformed into new creations that still retained the shared African heritage as their foundation. As George Ofari-Atta-Thomas explains:

> The African peoples, who were transported to the New World first and foremost brought with them their religion and worship heritage. Even in America, the African Religious heritage prevailed for 150 years before European-American Christianity significantly impacted the folk practices of Africans in this country. Their system of belief included: God-consciousness, the affirmation of a religious universe, prayer, corporate kinship in the vertical dimension (of past, present, and future) and in the horizontal dimensions (as the extended family-community relationship), spirit possession, immortality and the unity of reality, i.e., no separation between the sacred and the secular. Therefore, worship enhanced the connectedness of the whole being as one in touch with feelings, in the harmony of experience, in all existence.

These African inheritances were established in the Black religious heritage before, as stated above, European American Christianity affected the religious folk practices of Africans in America.[20]

A major reason for the perpetuation of African religious, social, and other mores was the above-mentioned failure of the slaveholders to introduce their slaves to Christianity, especially in an undistorted way, until well into the nineteenth century. Most Protestant slave owners feared that baptizing slaves would mean they could not continue to hold them as slaves because it had been historically taught, especially under English law, that a Christian could not enslave another Christian. In addition, many recognized the contradiction in teaching and preaching a religion that saw all of humanity as created by God while denying humanity to one race of human beings—those of African descent. It was only when the established churches, especially the Anglican Church in Virginia, decreed that conversion provided only a spiritual rather than actual physical freedom, that serious efforts at conversion of the slaves were made.[21] Even then, however, many still hesitated, fearing the consequences of preaching the gospel of Jesus to an enslaved people, especially in the aftermath of slave revolts (to be discussed later) instigated by Christian slaves. It was not until the Second Great Awakening that the evangelization of Africans in the South came to be seen as of value as a means of pacification for slaves inclined to question the rightness of their enslavement. As Charles Pinckney Jr. of South Carolina, a leading evangelist and politician of the time, noted:

> Were true religion propagated among this numerous and important class, a sense of duty would counteract their reluctance to labor, and diminishing the cases of feigned sickness so harassing to the Planter, would augment their numerical force and consequent production. The social relations of life being better observed, a greater

proportion of domestic happiness would prevail and render them more contented with their situation, and more anxious to promote their owner's welfare.[22]

Another prominent evangelist was Georgian Charles Colcock Jones (1804–63), who also believed that bad slaves could be turned into good ones through the proper implementation of Christian doctrine:

> The duty of obedience will never be performed to the extent that we desire it, unless we can *bottom it on religious principle.* That was the key. For if the blacks would come to believe that obedience to white owners was a religious duty, that submission to their masters was an obligation owed to God, then the authority of the planters would be built upon a solid rock.[23]

Jones argued for oral religious instruction of the slaves, promising that it would "provide economic advantages for slaveholders."[24] Drawing teachers from local slaveholders would guarantee, he believed, that only those understandings conducive to the slaves well-being and the owners' control would be taught. Although he insisted that the slaves' salvation was the primary goal of this instruction, for many owners, the incentive was purely economic self-interest.

Both Jones and Pinckney were greatly influenced by the egalitarian teachings of the newly formed Baptist and Methodist churches that emerged from the First and Second Great Awakenings and that led to the conversion of many, Black and white alike, often at the same time and place.[25] Although this freedom of worship did not last for the slaves, the revivals of religion had a significant impact.

> The revivalism of the Great Awakening, spread over time and space by evangelical preachers, created the conditions for large-scale conversion of the slaves. By revitalizing the religious piety of the South, the

Awakening(s) stirred an interest in conversion which was turned toward the slaves. By heavily emphasizing the inward conversion experience, the Awakening tended to de-emphasize the outward status of men and to cause Black and white alike to feel personally that Christ had died for them as individuals. Evangelical religion had a universalistic dimension which encouraged preaching to all men, embracing rich and poor, free and slave. The emotionalism and plain doctrine of revivalist preaching appealed to the masses, including the slaves.[26]

For most of those enslaved, exposure to Christianity brought about a number of changes in their lives. Affirmed by their masters, many became Christian in order, hopefully, to receive better treatment. This was especially the case in the North, both before and after the Revolutionary War, where many slaves petitioned both their owners and local courts, using the same arguments the colonists were themselves using to support their claims for freedom—and many were successful in doing so.[27] Lured by the story of Jesus, a poor carpenter's son who died for the salvation of all, they dared to wonder and, in time, assert that they too were included in Jesus' liberation promise. In the South, however, most slaves were required to sign a statement acknowledging that conversion to Christianity did not, in keeping with the teachings of Anglicanism, bring about physical freedom.

An Enslaved Understanding of Scripture

In the eighteenth and early nineteenth centuries Protestant slaves were often allowed to study the Bible, which was used as a means of teaching literacy. They absorbed the stories they found in both the Old and New Testaments. The Old Testament, with its vision of a wrathful yet wonderworking God who demanded justice and righteousness and fought on the side of God's people, was familiar to them, accustomed as they were to an omnipotent God who was quick to anger but who also loved all that God had created. The New Testament, with its tales of the journey of Jesus, who dared to take on the powers of his day and suffered a horrific death as a result of his courageous and challenging message to the poor, women, and all who were oppressed, was also familiar, for it seemed, in many ways, to parallel their own situation. Many were convinced that this God-man, Jesus, was on their side and understood their perilous situation.

The African people were an oral people who were able to retain massive amounts of their history, culture, and traditions as well as their religiosity without writing them down. This made for easier transmission of these retentions, especially and usually through the elders, but also through the mothers of children. On learning to read, they taught those around them to the best of their ability. As Allen Dwight Callahan affirms, the Bible, usually learned through oral rather than through written means, provided Africans with a means of bringing together Christianity and their preexisting religious worldview:

> American slaves did not read the Bible through, or even over and against, the traditions they brought with them from West Africa: they read the Bible as a text into which these traditions were woven. The characters and events of the Bible became the functional equivalent of the ancestors and heroes long celebrated in West Africa. The many ancestral spirits were subsumed in the Holy Spirit, and the mighty acts of God supplanted ancient tales of martial valor. Biblical patriarchs and heroes now sat on the stools of the esteemed ancestors of ages past.[28]

Thus, while ministers and masters, who were often one and the same, attempted to pacify the slaves, using a distorted understanding of Christianity as an opiate to dull their sense of self and their longing for freedom, the slaves themselves looked beyond this distorted message and found their own meaning in Christianity in ways we still do not fully understand. An example of this disjunction can be seen in the methodology often used by planters based on the writings of St. Paul, especially his Epistle to Philemon. Callahan notes:

> Certain scriptural texts were emphasized, such as Paul's Epistle to Philemon, and similar readings which stressed the duties of servant to master, the God-given mandate of obedience to one's superiors, and the necessity that one rest in the state in which one found oneself without agitating for a change in one's situation (cf. 1 Cor. 7:20–24; Eph 6:5–7, Titus 2:9), while others, especially any referring to liberation, were ignored or glossed over.[29]

Philemon, especially, was a favorite story used repeatedly to encourage slaves to remain in their divinely appointed places as evidence of their obedience to God's will. Dwight Hopkins affirms that "white planters employed the authority of the Bible in a self-serving and racist interpretation":

> Whites viewed slaves like other livestock. . . . God had created and intended for them to work for their white masters with a cheerful and loyal countenance. . . . The white man believed he replaced the mediating and liberating role of Jesus Christ. As the anointed Jesus, the white man possessed omnipotent and salvific capabilities. For black chattel to reach God, then, whites forced African Americans to accept the intermediary and divine status of the white race.[30]

Again, the result was a distortion of Christianity that emphasized the sacred world as a place of reward for "duties performed" over against a secular world of injustice and inhumanity. The situation of the slaves was glossed over and justified as the work of God who had condemned the African people because of the alleged sins of their ancestors to lives of perpetual and hellish servitude.

The slaves, however, did not accept without question or criticism the form of Christianity that their owners attempted to impose on them. Although some may have accepted some aspects of this passive and fatalistic Christianity, especially those who lived in close circumstances with them as servants, others completely rejected it, while still others, refusing to accept an interpretation of God and Jesus Christ that rendered them as less than human, instead absorbed those aspects that fit their self-understanding as a people created in the image and likeness of a God who loved them and was concerned about their well-being.

Thus, they developed their own liberating theology grounded in sacred scripture but read through the lens of their own lived experiences as slaves. Before their masters and ministers they usually sat in sullen submission to the preaching and exhortations, but there were also times when they protested verbally and physically the lies they believed they were being taught. Erskine Clarke tells of one leader who recalls:

> I was preaching to a large congregation on the Epistle of Philemon and when I insisted upon fidelity and obedience to Christian virtues in servants and upon the authority of Paul, condemned the practice of running away, one half of my audience deliberately rose up and walked off with themselves, and those that remained looked anything but satisfied either with the preacher or his doctrine.[31]

They often vigorously denied the minister's interpretation of scripture, especially if he was a slave owner himself, stating that such readings were not part of the true gospel message of Christ. "[This] meant these black slaves had a theological perspective to stand over against that of the whites, one which could provide them with an alternative to the 'religious principle' Jones had said was necessary."[32]

Many, both slave and free, refused to even consider Christianity with all of its negativity toward the body, especially the black body. White Christians taught that people of African descent were not human but only property and that their human form was a degraded aspect of the white form, which was seen as made in God's image; many even questioned whether they had souls. Those enslaved were denied any control over their physical bodies, which were beaten, whipped, burned, branded, starved, frozen, raped, and in numerous other ways abused and mistreated. This reluctance "signaled black people's determination to exercise a measure of agency over what they could in some respect control, their religious/ spiritual life. . . . They—black men and women—seized control over their own spirituality by steadfastly rejecting the form and message of Christianity as presented to them by Anglican [and other] missionaries,"[33] that is, a Christianity that affirmed slavery and the demonization of their very being. They denied specifically the validity of a Christianity that not only accepted but promoted their enslavement and also preached a message of conformity, passivity, and negativity regarding their very human selves.

As Kelly Brown Douglas observes:

> Informed by either the survival of ritualistic carryovers from their African religious traditions or first-hand memories, many black women and men maintained that a person's religiosity was defined by more than intellectual assent to certain rules and doctrines. Authentic spirituality—that is, a relationship to divine reality—was not a matter of the mind; it was rather a matter of the soul and body. This meant, then, that a person's spiritual condition—that is, the state of one's soul—and/or one's immediate relationship to divinity should be empirically evident through some form of bodily expression.[34]

This religious conviction on the part of the slaves, over time, led, not surprisingly, to a number of slave uprisings. These began as early as 1663 in New York and 1739 in South Carolina. They were usually instigated not by the rebellious field slaves who constantly balked at their situation but more often by the more privileged house slaves or artisans, including self-trained preachers whose numbers grew after the Second Great Awakening. It was believed by both Baptists and Methodists that slaves were better exhorters, not only of their own people, but of whites as well because of their fervent and emotional preaching. Their positions allowed them greater freedom of movement from plantation to plantation. Many of them had learned to write and read and had also been given permission to travel as Methodist or Baptist preachers. They believed deeply that God was offended by their enslavement and dehumanization and intended for them to be set free. As leaders of the Invisible Institution, the name by which the secret or hidden religious practices of the slaves was known—and the origin of the emerging Black Church in the South as experienced in brush arbors and slave cabins—these early Black ministers preached and proclaimed a God who hears the cries of the poor and oppressed and who, more important, responds to those cries with punitive action against those perpetuating such injustice.

The privilege of learning to read and write was eventually forbidden to the enslaved and made punishable by death on many Protestant plantations as the slaves increasingly used these skills not simply to rebel but to escape slavery. This restriction and other forms of the Black Codes that attempted to regulate and restrict every aspect of the lives of Blacks, both slave and free, beginning in the eighteenth century, were a response to the growing acceptance of perpetual servitude for Blacks as well as to the increasing number of rebellions led by enslaved Blacks who had learned to read and write and used their knowledge to escape. These efforts did not stop the slaves from passing on what knowledge and skills they had to those coming after them. As an oral people, the slaves handed down, from generation to generation, the knowledge needed to survive, the secrets of literacy, and other necessary and critical skills as a sacred treasure to be cherished, nurtured, and perpetuated.

John Lovell has pointed out that as Christian conversion increased among the slaves,

> the slave adopted the symbols of the Christian religion but not the hypocritical practices. He recalled that Christianity had introduced the slave traffic; that, as Linda Brent said, there was a great difference between religion and Christianity. . . . In many areas he accepted Christianity but only on his terms; he did not accept the white man's broken and bespattered Christianity. . . . It is true that many slaves by learning to read and other devices, learned about the Bible, Old Testament and New. And having learned, they taught their fellows. But the Bible acquired in this fashion was less religious doctrine and more the kind of pithy story the African had been used to for centuries.[35]

The clearest expression of the slaves' anti-European Christian understanding of Christianity, of their theology and spirituality, is revealed in their music, especially the spirituals or sorrow songs that later evolved into the blues, jazz, and today's gospel music. It is also, however, seen in their folktales, their prayers, their preaching, and their religious dance.

> Rather than a new religion, Christianity and its tradition of storytelling (especially in the Old Testament) represented primarily for those enslaved people a rich source of material, readily available to Africans from diverse pre-slavery backgrounds, for use in continuing in the new world the African tradition of song and dance, with storytelling and poetry at the center of the singing.[36]

These will be discussed in greater detail in Chapter 4. What becomes clear is that when the Africans and their descendants were finally formally introduced to Christianity, they were able to grasp its liberatory significance for themselves despite the distortions placed upon it by their masters. They asserted their own control over what they would and would not accept from the Christianity being given them, seeing through the lies and distortions their fellow white Christians sought to use to pacify and reduce them to a lower state of humanity or no humanity at all. They took this understanding to heart, and it became the source of a renewed African American spirituality that confounded many. Recognizing in Jesus Christ someone who had shared in their life of unjust oppression and suffering, they built a faith that, in time, would change the course of American history. How they did this is unclear. Somehow, an illiterate, oral people was able to grasp the kernel of truth of the Christian faith, that Jesus died to set all humans free, and to pass that belief down to the following generations to build further on and develop. Theirs was a paradoxical, "in spite of" faith that gave them the strength and courage to persevere in the face of horrible odds.

3

Say Amen, Somebody[1]

Emergence of African American Spirituality

*I have seen nothing nor heard nothing, but
only felt the spirit in my soul, and I believe
that will save me when I come to die.*
—GOD STRUCK ME DEAD: VOICES OF EX-SLAVES[2]

What is most amazing about the spirituality of African
Americans is the simple fact that it exists in spite of the myriad trials and tribulations they have experienced in the course
of their centuries-long sojourn in the United States. Yet the
story does not end merely with the existence of a particular
form of spirituality. It is necessary to examine how and why
African slaves were able to persevere as people of faith in such
conditions. This means looking not only at the origins of African American spirituality and its African roots, as we have
done in preceding chapters, but also at how that spirituality
has been expressed and experienced over those centuries. It
means going deeper into their experiences of God, experiences
that go beyond their rudimentary and too often negative
introduction to the Christian faith. Those enslaved knew the
difference between meaningless and soulless rites and rituals
that did not sustain life and a true encounter with God that
could change an individual in myriad ways. As Calvin Bruce
affirms, "African American spirituality, in its very essence,
is African-based, against white racism, and the source of

inspiration for the black community's struggle toward freedom."[3] He notes that many use the terms *African American religion* and *African American spirituality* interchangeably, but in actuality spirituality is not synonymous with religion.

In *Resurrection Song: African American Spirituality*, Flora Wilson Bridges describes the difference:

> Religion essentially involves the institutionalization of rites, rituals, and dogmas [making it] possible for human beings to be religious without experiencing God and responding to God's call to participate in community. . . .
>
> Spiritual identity . . . is the result of an actual encounter with the Divine wherein the human being cannot bypass participation in what [can be called] a "transpersonal ultimacy" that requires the person to live out actual values that foster true community. Religion teaches humankind to appreciate God's love; but spirituality challenges human beings to directly experience the transformative power of God's love. Religion is a belief system or reflection on the nature of ultimate reality. Spirituality is the method and manner by which the ultimately real actually touches the depth of being of the human personality, transforms it, and causes it to long for true community. Religion may enlighten the mind, but spirituality converts the entire existence.[4]

African Americans are a spiritual people who are also religious. It is their spirituality, however, which stands at the center of their very being, that has enabled them to become a people of Christian faith, a faith very different from that of white Christians in the United States. Their spirituality, one that emphasizes resistance, survival, and liberation, freed them to become the people God intended them to be rather than personal property, as others saw them.

African American spirituality is firmly rooted in the slaves' experience of and encounter with the all-encompassing power of the Spirit. The African understanding of *ntu*, the spiritual life force, was transferred to the Christian understanding of the Holy Spirit who, like *ntu*, sustains and nurtures the living and connects them with those who have gone on before—the ancestors—as well as with all creation.

According to Robert Hood,

> The Spirit experientially and conceptually exercises a very strong influence in black American religion and culture. . . . Like the breath of God in Scripture, this power marks the slave songs and gospel hymns, the rhetoric of the black preacher and the black trickster alike, the extemporaneous and unrehearsed prayers of the unsophisticated, and the written liturgical prayers of more sedate congregations. It is the presence of the Spirit—revealed in the sounds and ritual of black churches—that impresses black folk at a service, prayer meeting, Bible class, or a revival. With the Spirit present they can say with great sagacity and joy that they really are a "church" and are in "spirit-filled worship."[5]

Spirit Possession and Being Slain in the Spirit

The ring shout is one of the clearest examples of how the slaves adapted and reinterpreted African traditions over time and generations and merged them with Christian religious expressions to form a unique expression that, for them, was healing, holy, and liberating. Its origins are African, and it was danced by slaves in the West Indies and the United States. When exactly the traditional African religious dances became a part of the religious worship of those enslaved is unclear. It was a gradual merging of memory and music that enabled those enslaved to worship God and stay in communion with the ancestors.[6] As Raboteau notes, "While the North American slaves danced under the impulse of the Spirit of a 'new' God, they danced in ways their fathers in Africa would have recognized."[7] The ring shout was an important means of building community among the slaves. Those who shared a common oppression were invited into its circle, and for them the revolving circle of singers, moaners, and shouters provided a spiritual as well as an emotional release from everyday life. The ring shout was undeniably African in its origins and used the same motions, actions, and movements that had been used in African rituals:

> [It consists of] a circle of people moving single file (usually counter-clockwise) around a central point, to the accompaniment of singing, stamping, and heel clicking. In some instances, the participants tap (in effect, drum) on the floor rhythmically with sticks to produce percussive effects. The steps are akin to a shuffle, with free foot movement prohibited, and little versatility permitted. Sometimes, the clearly defined single file gives way to a sort of amorphous crowd moving around a central point. The tempo may build up gradually, singing interspersed with exclamations . . . until it reaches a tense peak close to an ecstatic breaking point. At the high point of the excitement, such exclamations as "Oh, Lord!" and "Yes, Lord" turn into nonsense sounds and cries; seemingly wild emotional responses, they nevertheless are related to the music as a whole, and no notation which omits them can give a fair picture of what is heard.[8]

However, as those enslaved became better acquainted with Christianity, changes did take place. As Raboteau notes, "the 'holy dance' of the shout may very well have been a two-way bridge connecting the core of West African religions—possession by the gods—to the core of evangelical Protestantism—the experience of conversion."[9]

It is in the ring shout that we also encounter another important aspect of African American spirituality—that of being "slain in the Spirit"—which has its roots in the African experience of "spirit possession." However, the two, although sharing many similarities, are not the same. A discontinuity can be said to exist "between the African heritage of spirit possession and the black shouting tradition in the United States." Yet, a distinctive continuity exists as well "in the context of action, the patterns of motor behavior preceding and following the ecstatic experience."[10]

Both traditions involve "hand-clapping, foot-tapping, rhythmic preaching, hyperventilation, antiphonal (call and response) singing and dancing."[11] In the United States only the drums were missing initially because it was illegal for a slave on Protestant plantations to possess drums. These were, however, very present in Catholic colonies such as Louisiana where connections between African and African American religiosity were more easily maintained. After slavery's end, drums reemerged, along with brass and wind instruments, guitars, piano, organ, tambourines, and other instrumental forms of "making a joyful noise unto the Lord" (Psalm 100) in the Protestant congregations. Meanwhile, ironically, they began to fade in Catholic ones until their reemergence in the mid-twentieth century. The "circle" or "ring" dance of African tradition gradually over time was merged into the "ring shout" of Christianized African Americans. It is still practiced today in the Sea Islands.

It was in their own "invisible institution," exemplified by the "hush/brush arbors," that the slaves were free to create their own vehicles to express the Spirit and gain the strength to persevere. These "arbors" were places hidden in the woods and other locations on the plantations, such as caves, where those enslaved could celebrate and worship without, hopefully, the masters hearing and disrupting them. Here it was that the field hollers, work songs, sorrow songs, spirituals, and even the blues had their origins as the slaves recovered their sense of sacred being through songs, ritual, music, and dance. It is within these sacred spaces that the ring shout was melded and molded into a Christian expression of faith and worship of the Christian God. In this truly spiritual experience they testified and witnessed to their faith and shared those testimonies with one another, laying the foundations for a community of believers who were touched by God.

As the Black church began to coalesce in these hush/brush arbor gatherings and slowly emerge in institutional forms organized by Blacks themselves[12] in the late eighteenth and early nineteenth centuries, we see a continuation of the ecstatic experience of the ring shout displayed in response to fervent preaching and emotive singing. Albert Raboteau gives a moving example of this experience:

> The preacher was drawing his sermon to a close . . . when a small old woman . . . among those in the gallery, suddenly rose and began dancing and clapping her hands; at first with a slow and measured movement, and then with increasing rapidity, at the same time beginning to shout "ha! ha!" The women about her arose also, and tried to hold her. . . . The woman was still shouting and dancing, her head thrown back and rolling from one side to the other. Gradually her shout became indistinct, she threw her arms wildly about instead of clapping her hands, fell back into the arms of her companions, then threw herself forward and embraced those before her, then tossed herself from side to side, gasping, and finally sunk to the floor, where she remained . . . kicking, as if acting a death struggle.[13]

On a physical level the traditions of spirit possession and being slain in the spirit may be seen as similar, especially when viewing one of the Afro-Catholic religious rituals. On the level of theological interpretation they are interpreted differently. In the African tradition, devotees of a particular god or gods are possessed by that god or those gods "whose personality displaces that of the human medium which has no self-control." However, in Black Christianity, it is "the context of belief [that] shapes the possession experience and determines the manner in which the experience is interpreted."[14] Depending on the tradition the human is "mounted" and "rode" by a god or gods (African), or it is instead "the Holy Spirit who fills the converted sinner with a happiness and power that drives him to shout, sing and sometimes dance."[15] An ex-slave preacher spoke of his own experiences in these gatherings as follows:

> The old Meetinghouse caught on fire. The spirit was there. Every heart was beating in unison as we turned our minds to God to tell him of our sorrows here below. God saw our need and came to us. I used to wonder what made people shout but now I don't. There is a joy on the inside and it wells up so strong that we can't keep still. It is fire in the bones. Any time that fire touches a man, he will jump.[16]

The Conversion Experience: Protestant

As discussed in Chapter 2, serious efforts to convert the slaves did not begin until after the First Great Awakening in the eighteenth century and did not really have a significant impact upon the slaves until the Second Great Awakening early in the nineteenth century. However, when finally allowed to convert, they did so with great enthusiasm, finding in Christianity, arguably, an answer to many fervent prayers.

It is the belief, the faith context, that is essentially different for African American Christians, especially those enslaved. This is most clearly seen in the narrative of the slaves themselves as they recount their conversion experiences. Again, although the African slaves were taught a distorted Christianity that mandated their oppression and denied their humanity, they were able, paradoxically, to discern the kernel of truth in Jesus' message: God is a God for all and all of God's creation is good. Their conversion experiences compounded this goodness within them in ways that dramatically contrasted their physical status of enslavement with their spiritual breaking of the chains that bound them. The indwelling of the Spirit within them freed them to become who they were meant to be, liberating them from the chains of slavery and everyday toil and taking them to a higher place.

For the slaves, to be converted meant "getting religion," being "slain in the spirit," or being "struck dead" by the hand of God and revived as a new being. It was a physical experience, active rather than passive, in which the Holy Spirit invaded the physical being of the slaves, leading them to shout; speak of visions of God, heaven, or freedom; and engage in often frenzied behavior that manifested the Spirit's presence. Theirs was not an intellectual conversion, a meeting of minds, but a meeting of hearts and souls that transformed their lives forever.

In keeping with their African ancestors they experienced an ontic change, a profound transformation that called them forth as new beings in Christ, cleansed and refreshed, looking all new, having lost their former selves and been reborn. One's true rather than enslaved identity was revealed through conversion, the revelation that one was a child of God, a human being, one of the redeemed of God, and it is the Spirit of the Lord Jesus Christ who showed the path to that new identity. George Cummings notes:

> The Spirit's presence . . . entailed the affirmation of independence and selfhood, sustained hope for freedom as embodied in their prayer life; served as the basis of love within the slave community; and even assisted slaves in their desire to escape to freedom. The Spirit's sustaining power/presence was nurtured in the secret meetings where black slaves disobeyed their masters' orders to serve God, sustained their sense of personal identity and well-being, and provided mutual support for each other by giving meaning and hope to the tragic experience.[17]

Sarah Rhodes, a former slave, speaks of those meetings in this way: "We used to steal off to de woods and have church, like the spirit moved us—singing and praying to our own liking and soul satisfaction—and we sure did have good meetings, honey—baptize in de river like God said. We had dem spirit-filled meetings at night on de bank of de river and God met us there."[18]

It was often at nighttime that conversions took place, but they could also happen anywhere and anytime—in the fields, in the shacks, even in the presence of whites. Harriet Tubman's experience of conversion speaks to the heart of the change felt by the newly born or reborn Christian. Tubman speaks of an experience seemingly physically as well as spiritually transformative when she escaped to freedom in the North, an experience that transformed her into the "liberator" of her people. She states that it was immediately after stepping onto free land in the North that she realized that God had given her a specific mission, which was to free her family and as many others as she could.

> The moment she stepped into free territory and consecrated herself to the mission of rescuing her family and friends, a great change took place. "When I found I had crossed that line," she said, "I looked at my hands to see if I was the same person. There was such a glory over everything; the sun came like gold through the trees, and over the fields, and I felt like I was in Heaven. . . . I had crossed the line. I was free."[19]

Theirs was a defiance born of the Spirit, which moved them to disobey their masters in order to obey their God, a God they knew had created them as free men and women in God's own image and likeness. This Spirit-grounded strength enabled them to flee plantations and to plot and carry out escapes and rebellions while silently but obstinately refusing to participate in their own dehumanization, often to the consternation and fear of their masters, as shall be seen.

In discussions of Black/African American spirituality, two significant groups are often overlooked, namely, Black women and Black Roman Catholics. Both have contributed and continue to contribute significantly to the emergence and ongoing development of the spirituality of persons of African descent in the United States. African American women's spirituality will be discussed in Chapter 7 of this work.

The Conversion Experience: Roman Catholic

Lest we think the events of the Great Awakening were restricted to slaves on Protestant plantations, it is necessary also to look at the experiences of Catholic slaves. Present in the Catholic Church since the earliest beginnings of Christianity, Blacks also participated actively in Christianity's revival spirit. Most were, as noted earlier, part of the French-speaking and Spanish-speaking churches, but in the English-speaking colonies the great majority were found in Maryland, where they were owned by Catholics, including clergy and religious. One of the largest slaveholders on the Eastern seaboard was the Jesuit order, which established large tobacco plantations throughout southern Maryland to support its itinerant ministry, leaving the everyday running to the slaves themselves.[20] Although we do not know the numbers of slaves who were already Catholic when they were brought to the United States, we know many persevered in their faith unless forced to convert to the faith of their owners on Protestant plantations.

African slaves, as noted, found themselves attracted to Catholicism. For many, its teachings and, more important, its rites and rituals reminded them of their own indigenous religious traditions. Roman Catholicism was more open to the survival of African religious beliefs and ritual practices than Protestantism. At the same time, it is often claimed that the more emotive expressions, such as "prayer meetings, shouting and spirituals—the staples of Black Protestantism—were often foreign to the experience of Black Catholics because of the Catholic church's insistence on more staid and sober rituals."[21] This is not, however, completely true.

Although some Catholic slaves were certainly influenced by the Methodist and Baptist revivals, they also had their own conversion experiences within the Roman Catholic Church. Because of the small number of ordained priests in the United States and the great distances they were required to travel through huge dioceses to far-flung parishes, Catholic priests, like their brother Baptist and Methodist ministers, were itinerant ministers. They spent weeks and even months on horseback, traveling from one settlement to another, bringing, often belatedly, the sacraments to those who had gone without for months and sometimes years.

Roman Catholic slaves found themselves in situations similar to those of Protestants. The Bible was not available to them as a literacy tool because it was in Latin, and they did not have access to ordained priests of their own race because these did not emerge until the end of the nineteenth century.[22] Yet they too remembered the stories read to them from the Bible and recognized the voice of liberation crying out in their wilderness. Many, however, especially in the French-speaking and Spanish-speaking Catholic colonies, were able to become literate because skilled slaves were used as artisans, house servants, teachers, and concubines. Many Catholic slaves, biracial because of illegal but accepted liaisons with French and Spanish owners who did not deny their humanity or their own paternity, as was more often done in Protestant colonies, served as the foundation for what became the free people of color *(gens libres de couleur)*, especially in the New Orleans area. They formed an independent group of faith-filled Catholics of color who worshiped alongside their white brothers and sisters and participated in society, albeit at a lower level. They helped to form a Black Catholic spirituality rooted in the Latin mass and, in the popular Catholicism of the people, a culture that encouraged syncretism of Catholic beliefs with still-present African traditions, especially Yoruba. The result was the emergence in the Caribbean and Latin America of distinct Afro-Catholic religions (Vodoun,

Santería, and Candomblé) that also existed in the lower South, especially after the Haitian revolution (1791–1804).

During and after slavery, as discussed earlier, Black Protestants were greatly influenced by the teachings of the Methodist and Baptist churches that broke away from the Anglican Church seeking a "freer" expression of faith and an openness to God for persons at all levels of society, not just the elite. The Second Great Awakening was especially critical because it led to a sense of social reform among Protestants, resulting in efforts such as those of Charles Colcock Jones (discussed in Chapter 2).

> By heavily emphasizing the inward conversion experience, the Awakening tended to de-emphasize the outward status of men, and to cause black and white alike to *feel* personally that Christ had died for them as individuals. Evangelical religion had a universalistic dimension which encouraged preaching to all men, embracing rich and poor, free and slave. The emotionalism and plain doctrine of revivalist preaching appealed to the masses, including the slaves.[23]

What is not so well known, however, is the impact of this "opening to the Spirit" on Roman Catholics in the United States in the nineteenth century. As noted before, while Baptist and Methodist itinerant ministers on horseback traveled for miles to far-flung parts of the nation to hold revivals that brought thousands into their folds, a similar practice was developed by Catholic priests, especially those in the Jesuit, Paulist, and Redemptorist orders. They too traveled around the country on horseback in order to proclaim the gospel and celebrate the sacraments with the faithful, who often did not see a priest for months on end.

Although never called a revival until the latter part of the nineteenth century, many slaves in Catholic plantations and, more important, in urban areas were taught the basics of their faith by means of the parish mission, a revival in all but name. It soon became clear that assertive action was needed to prevent "backsliding" among the Catholic faithful, Black and white alike. The Paulists, the first Catholic religious order founded in the United States (1858), came into existence precisely to provide for the spiritual and sacramental needs of fellow Catholics. The result of their efforts was the parish mission. It was preached with powerful emotion, with the congregation often responding with spontaneous outbursts of weeping, shuddering, and moaning.

Conceived in Europe in the sixteenth and seventeenth centuries, the parish mission was a response to a growing religious malaise among clergy and congregations. Exported to the United States these missions served admirably as a vehicle both for evangelization and for reviving the faith of those who had been unable to participate in church services because of distance and other obstacles. The missions initiated a new style of preaching that exhorted the faithful with scenes of hellfire and imminent damnation.

The similarities to Protestant camp meetings were striking in many ways. Both took place in locations where large groups could be assembled in tents or barns. Both sought the conversion of participants and the reclamation of sinners for Christ. The spoken word was stressed, often accompanied by a variety of theatrical techniques to induce the sinner to repent and return to the fold. Preachers known for their exhortatory fervor labored long and hard to remind the faithful of their sinful nature and the sinful state they were in and called upon them to repent and "get right" with God.

A significant difference in the parish mission, however, was that it emphasized not only individual conversion but also the reception of the sacraments and participation in the mass as proof of being saved. In the words of historian Jay P. Dolan:

> A mission . . . is something which gathers into one powerful showing all the warnings of Divine Justice fully explaining the enormous folly and ingratitude of sin; it leads the sinner back to his very childhood and traces his

downward track through youth and manhood towards
his last death; which stands with him at his open grave;
which calls in the ear the summons to the judgment seat
of an offended God; which scorches his face with the
fires of hell and all in an atmosphere of fervor, aided
by the entreaties of the sinner's friends, their prayers
to God, their tears, the example of the repentance of
other sinners.[24]

Jesuits and Paulists, as noted, were leaders in promoting
parish missions, especially "out west" in the wilds of Ken-
tucky and Ohio. Many noted the significance and appeal of
these missions to the lives and spirituality of Black Catholics,
recognizing their desire for a more spirit-filled experience of
God to encourage their continued participation. Just as during
and after the Protestant Awakenings when Blacks and whites
worshiped together in Christian solidarity, Catholics joined
with one another to feel the Spirit moving within their midst
and in themselves, urging them to confess their sins, repent,
and be united with the love of God and the communion of
saints once again.

Thus, for many Black Catholics, the Catholic parish mission became a source of renewal and revival. They were
exposed to the fervent exhortation and the Spirit-filled
conversion experience of revivals in two ways. They either
attended a mission within the parish (the great majority) or
stole away to the meetings of the Black Protestant church
(or sometimes did both). Regardless of the source, however,
even after revivalism began to wane, the seed had been sown
from which a Black Catholic spirituality would emerge that,
over time, became as rich, community-building, supportive,
and soul-satisfying as Black Protestant spirituality. It was
and continues to be a spirituality that sustained Black culture
in the Catholic communities and led in the mid-twentieth
century to the emergence of a distinctive Black Catholic
worship style.[25]

Slave Resistance

Slave resistance (rather than revolt or rebellion) involved more than bloody rebellions against slaveholders, although a number of these did take place, especially by those who interpreted God's message as calling for the liberation of those enslaved by any means necessary. Resistance in other forms included running away, singly or in groups; acting counter to the masters' commands; sabotaging tools, farm equipment, crops, and other property; "going slow" as often and as much as possible; and holding their own religious services (hush arbors or brush arbors) where they could listen to their own preach a radically different gospel message. What is clear is that "the African American people, in slavery, forged a record of discontent and of resistance comparable to that marking the history of any oppressed people."[26]

Fear of slave insurrections and rebellions was rampant in every area of the United States (and the colonies prior to its founding) where slavery existed. Although for decades historians argued that those enslaved were happy and contented beings, the reality is much different. Historian Herbert Aptheker was the first to denounce the accepted view that those enslaved were happy and contented in their enslavement. His seminal work, *American Negro Slave Revolts*, revealed the long and often violent history of African Americans' resistance to their captivity, which began with the first Africans brought in chains to these shores and continued until slavery was abolished in the aftermath of the Civil War. Although we have in-depth records of only a few, there is more than sufficient collateral evidence to reveal that discontent as it was played out in the communities where those enslaved lived and worked. This discontent was fostered by their conversion to Christianity, a Christianity of resistance and liberation.

Encouraged by their understanding of sacred scripture and its revolutionary message of liberation set forth particularly

in the Gospels as it had been handed down through generations, the enslaved saw Jesus as the one who sets all people
free, who rights their wrongs, and who opposes their enslavement. The Gospels were supplemented by readings from the
Hebrew scriptures that emphasized God's action in human
history—as in Exodus and the Prophets—in setting free those
wrongly oppressed.

Many of those who had access to the Bible and were therefore somewhat literate, especially those Blacks who had been
allowed to become Methodist or Baptist ministers, exhorters,
and evangelists in the early 1800s, used their capabilities to
arouse as much dissension in the ranks of their people as they
could. Men like Nat Turner (1831), Denmark Vesey (1822),
Gabriel Prosser (1800), and Cato (Jemmy, 1739) felt called
by God and guided by their faith to end their and others'
enslavement, exchanging it for a hard-fought-for freedom.

The earliest of these rebellions took place in 1739 at the
Stono River in South Carolina. It was the first that we know
of to be organized by Roman Catholic slaves (an earlier possible insurrection took place in New York City, allegedly led by
a Catholic priest in 1712), who were predominantly Kongo.
Maintaining the faith they had acquired in their homeland,
they were particularly open to the enticements of the Spanish,
who were at that time engaged in conflict with the American
colonists and who promised land and freedom to any slaves
that left the Carolinas for Florida. Finding themselves on
plantations run by Protestants, they determined to continue
the practice of their faith and to escape their enslavement.
John Thornton notes:

> South Carolina slaves were in all likelihood . . . drawn
> from . . . the kingdom of Kongo [in modern Angola],
> which was a Christian country and had a fairly extensive
> system of schools and churches in addition to a high
> degree of literacy . . . in Portuguese. . . . The Kongolese
> were proud of their Christian and Catholic heritage,
> which they believed made them a distinctive people,

and thus Kongolese slaves would have seen the Spanish offers in terms of freedom of religion, or rather, freedom of Catholic religion as additionally attractive beyond promises of freedom in general.[27]

Their awareness of the Gregorian calendar led them, it is believed, to plan their revolt on the day of the Virgin Mary's birth and to instigate it the following day, a Sunday. Although unsuccessful, it shows the strength, resilience, and faith of these freedom fighters who believed strongly in the unfairness of their situation. Historian Mark Smith has done a detailed study of the Catholic influence on this revolt:

> [The slaves] revolted when they did [September 9, 1739] because of their specific veneration of the Virgin Mary, their general commitment to and understanding of the Catholic calendar observed in the Kongo, and because their temporal understanding of that calendar had necessarily undergone a silent (but ultimately incidental) transformation in their forced relocation to a predominantly Protestant plantation society.[28]

Later acts of violent resistance organized by Protestant slaves were grounded in the same sense of injustice at their situation. Turner, Vesey, and Prosser all believed they had been called and anointed by God to free their people. These actions, bloody though they were, were rooted in a faith in a God who sided with those unjustly oppressed, a God who opposed their enslavement and empowered them to rebel.

There are little or no known revolts led by women, but that did not mean they acquiesced in their servile state. Many formulated plans to escape and, like Harriet Tubman, saw their actions as consecrated by God. Others escaped as individuals or in other ways and used their freedom to agitate for the end of slavery, as did Harriet Jacobs. Black women utilized other forms of resistance available to them, using their knowledge of herbs, for example, both to heal their fellow slaves and to harm their masters, and using their often closer relationships to their owners as cooks and other types of domestic servants to foment rebellion. Their ability at quilting, according to some oral history, was a source of information and guidance for escaping slaves who read the signals embedded in the different quilt patterns and thus knew if it was safe to move on.[29]

Slave Narratives

It is the slave narratives, most of which were composed and published after slavery's end (and the great majority not until the 1930s), that reveal the eschatological hope of the enslaved, a hope that was reflective of a connection between the presence of the Spirit of God and the hopes and aspirations of the slave community.[30] Theirs was a hope born of their burning desire for freedom and their determination to one day be free. It was an eschatological hope born of the Spirit's movement within them and its sustaining and nurturing presence in every aspect of their lives. The slave narratives are a rich source for research on the religious faith and spirituality of African American slaves. They reveal the experiential loss of being and the reclamation of that being and its maintenance through faith in a liberating God. The narratives are also a mine of information about the ways in which those enslaved fought against and resisted the restrictions and limitations placed on them as sentient human beings. They show how the slaves' interpretation of God was very different from that of the slaveholders, male and female, and how they were inspired by that understanding to struggle for their freedom. Dwight Hopkins affirms this, noting that

> the slaves' faith in freedom never died, even in the face of an apparent everlasting evil. The slaves maintained their humanity with a steadfast hope in liberation as their ultimate concern. Some African American chattel fought individually. Others organized collectively. Some simply packed up and ran north to "Canaan."

Still others gave up any idea of achieving heaven on earth in their lifetime and waited for death to transport them across Jordan to see their Maker. . . . But, rarely, if at all, do we discover any enslaved African American equating, and thereby justifying, the demonic nature of slavery with the Bible or God's will and purpose for humanity. And it is in black chattel's faith in God's free intent for humanity that a universal note sounds in our ears. Despite what the slavery world said, God had a plan for all human beings, black and white, slave and free, to share the earth equally in freedom.[31]

As stated above, those enslaved read the Bible in very different ways from their captors, influenced both by their ancestral past and its traditions and their present experiences of bondage. Rather than adhering to the Letters of Paul—especially the story of Onesimus, the returned slave—and other scriptural affirmations that slavery was legitimate in the eyes of God, they read and studied the Book of Exodus and the Gospels. Seeing themselves as God's newly chosen people, wrongly enslaved against their will, they believed that God was acting in their history to overcome their present blighted state and achieve their freedom.

The slaves, buoyed up by their faith, looked forward to a reversal of the status quo, a shift in time and situation for them and those who oppressed them expressed in the belief that, as the spiritual states, "everybody talking about heaven ain't going there." The future was promised them and gave them the ability to stay strong, but it was not a future way off somewhere. It was at one and the same time here but also not yet in its fullness; the "home over yonder" and the "promised land" they sang about in the spirituals may have been seen as an otherworldly promise to some, but for the slaves they were a "this worldly" hope in a freedom soon to come. This was also seen in the slave rebellions that took place throughout the centuries of slavery, especially soon after Christianity was introduced to them in the Southern states.

A Paradoxical Faith

This steadfast faith in a God of justice and righteousness, in Jesus as liberator of those unjustly enslaved and oppressed, and in the Holy Spirit who gave them strength for the journey toward freedom enabled the transformation of Africans into African Americans, both Protestant and Roman Catholic. Their experience of God in the hellish furnace of slavery in the United States forged a new people, a faith-filled people, from the diverse peoples of West and Central Africa. Recognizing in themselves a kinship fostered by their experience of dehumanization, they emerged as a stalwart community of faith that stood in solidarity in the face of the many injurious forces arrayed against them. African Americans (colored, Negroes, Blacks)—this new people—persisted in their faith largely due to their paradoxical ability to see beyond their present reality to God's reality, when they all would be free not only in heaven but on earth as well. This belief, this theology of survival, liberation, and hope, was expressed, as Chapter 4 will reveal, most clearly in song, in the spirituals or sorrow songs and gospels that flowed from them in later years. These songs spoke of their pain and suffering but also revealed their ability to find joy and hope. They are the earliest expressions of African American God-talk, that is, Black theologizing.

Whether Protestant or Catholic, the communities of slaves were able, despite the restrictions placed upon them by owners and society, to create a place of refuge for themselves within the Christian religion. Refusing to accept the negative perspectives and teachings of white Christians, who sought by these means to subdue and pacify them, the slaves were able to find a firm foundation in Christ that enabled them not merely to survive but to persevere in their constant struggle for emancipation. In so doing, in their praise and worship, they were able to sing a new people into life.

4

Yet Do I Marvel

An Oral Spirituality

I doubt not God is good, well-meaning, kind.
. . .
Yet do I marvel at this curious thing,
To make a poet black, and bid him sing!
—Countee Cullen[1]

As an oral rather than literate people,[2] it is understandable that the slaves, regardless of faith, did not describe their faith in God, Jesus, and the Holy Spirit in books or other written forms. Rather, it was preserved in their hearts and souls and passed down orally in many different forms, enriched, embellished, and often transformed into new creations as needs arose. Music in the form of song, both solo and groups, was a central aspect of their lives and regardless of their occupation or situation, they expressed their joys and sorrows in field hollers, work songs, and, as the influence of Christianity grew among them, the sorrow songs or spirituals. These songs were the best example of this ability to "speak" their faith into action.

They sought "to maintain unity and to affirm identity" in this strange new land and did so by substituting the Christian God for the African High God. This was a fairly simple transition, as the seemingly new concept of a supreme god was in actuality not new to the transplanted Africans. This new but also familiar God became central, especially to ring rituals, with Christ substituting for all the divinities. Thus, in the ring shout and other such rituals, Christ, not the African gods, "rode" the participants.[3]

Albert Raboteau affirms that for those slaves introduced to Roman Catholicism, "Catholic notions about the role of Christ, Mary, guardian angels, and patron saints as intercessors with the Father in heaven for men on earth proved quite compatible with African ideas about the intervention of lesser gods in the day-to-day affairs of human life, while the supreme god remained benevolent and providential but distant."[4] Samuel A. Floyd Jr. also affirms this:

> This African-Catholic syncretism made the transition for Africans to Western culture easier . . . in some parts of the United States, particularly New Orleans, and served as support for the continuation of African religions in the New World. But it was Protestantism that fueled the religion and religious fervor of enslaved and free blacks in the United States. Protestantism, with its more direct access to the High God through song and praise, made possible the emergence of a new song for Africans, a new song in which they could express themselves as freely as they had in their homeland. This new song was the African-American spiritual.[5]

The Sorrow Songs

Although this body of songs was not fully written down until after the Civil War, they can be traced back into the seventeenth and eighteenth centuries as those enslaved became acquainted with various forms of Christianity. We have no dates or authors/composers, as they were passed down orally and often changed along the way to fit different circumstances. The same melody could have several different sets of lyrics. They varied in number, content, and even texts, based on the particular needs and concerns of those singing them from region to region, especially in the slaveholding South. These songs, better than anything else, reveal to us the spirituality of the slaves, their self-understanding, their understanding of God, their belief in Jesus, and their hope in the action of the Holy Spirit to help them stay in the race until freedom came. W. E. B. Du Bois evokes both the spiritual and liberative aspects of these songs:

Through all the sorrow of the Sorrow Songs there breathes a hope—a faith in the ultimate justice of things. The minor cadences of despair change often to triumph and calm confidence. Sometimes it is faith in life, sometimes a faith in death, sometimes assurance of boundless justice in some fair world beyond. But whichever it is, the meaning is always clear: that sometime, somewhere, men will judge men by their souls and not their skins. Is such a hope justified? Do the Sorrow Songs sing true?[6]

Yes, they do "sing true." As we explore the critical role that the spirituals have played in the development of African American spirituality, we realize that these songs were truly an extension of the very being of those enslaved. The songs speak to our hearts and souls because they came from the hearts and souls of a people who, with no foreseeable viable future, should have given in to despair and defeat. Instead, they rallied around Jesus Christ, as their brother and son, and the God of Creation, their father in heaven, and poured out their hopes and dreams, their fears and sorrows. In so doing they not only created a body of music that continues to bring solace to many today but they also built a new community, using these songs as brick and mortar, as pathways on their journey to freedom.

One song in particular, although believed to be composed only in the mid 1800s, affirms the ability of the slaves to take ordinary passages from scripture and weave out of them a passionate song of solidarity in faith and resistance. Over two millennia earlier, in another land, Jeremiah, a prophet of the Hebrew people, raised a troubling question. Confronted with the loss of their land, their culture, and their traditions, the prophet Jeremiah asked: "Is there no balm in Gilead?" (Jer 8:22). Gilead was a country known for its medicinal and healing balms, but there apparently were none that could satisfy the needs or heal the pain of the exiled Hebrew people. Centuries later and worlds away another people, enslaved and dehumanized as the Hebrews had been, raised Jeremiah's question yet again—but with a significant difference. They not only raised the same question, "Is there no balm in Gilead?" but paradoxically they also answered it in the affirmative, proclaiming in a spiritual:

> There is a balm in Gilead
> To make the wounded whole
> There is a balm in Gilead
> To heal the sin-sick soul.

This ability to take stories and sayings from scripture and bring them to life for the benefit of ordinary people is at the foundation of the paradoxical faith of Black American Christians.

The Role of the Spirituals: Compensatory or Revolutionary?

For almost a century after the end of slavery, the spirituals were considered "sorrow songs," compensatory plaints that enabled the slaves to sustain themselves in their despicable situations. They were understood as "cries to heaven" by helpless people putting their faith in a far-off heaven in order to maintain their human dignity in the present hell in which they passed their daily lives.

The two major purveyors of this rather passive view were W. E. B. Du Bois and Benjamin Mays, two early twentieth-century leaders in the Black community. Their explorations of the Negro's God and the Negro's church (Mays) and of the spiritual strivings of Black folk (Du Bois) provide us with a record of the contradictory ways in which those who were enslaved expressed their pain and suffering spiritually. Du Bois writes:

> We the darker ones come even now not altogether empty-handed: there are today no truer exponents of the pure human spirit of the Declaration of Independence than the American Negroes; there is no true American music but the wild sweet melodies of the Negro slave; the American fairytales and folk-lore are Indian and African; and, in all, we black men seem the sole oasis of simple faith and reverence in a dusty oasis of dollars and smartness. . . . The spiritual strivings of the freedmen's sons is the travail of souls whose burden is almost beyond the measure of their strengths, but who bear it in the name of an historic race, in the name of this land of their fathers' fathers, and in the name of human opportunity.[7]

While affirming the spiritual grounding from which these songs developed, Du Bois also affirms their originality:

> Little of beauty has America given to the world . . . ; the human spirit in this New World has expressed itself in vigor and ingenuity rather than in beauty. And so by fateful chance the Negro folk-song—the rhythmic cry of the slave—stands today not simply as the sole American music, but as the most beautiful expression of human experience born this side of the seas. It has been neglected, despised and above all it has been persistently mistaken and misunderstood; but not withstanding, it still remains as the singular spiritual heritage of the nation and the greatest gift of the Negro people.[8]

Songs such as "Steal Away" (to be discussed below), "Give Me Jesus," "I Couldn't Hear Nobody Pray," or "Go Down, Moses" are clearly songs that emerged from the very souls of an oppressed but not defeated people, who always saw their goal as freedom; they were resting in the Lord until the right time came. Many of these songs were a response to and source of information for those escaping slavery and referred directly to the Underground Railroad and other escape routes ("The Gospel Train's A Comin'," "Swing Low, Sweet Chariot," "Steal Away") while others warned of hardships ahead ("Wade in the Water"). Others spoke of their frustration and exhaustion at having to fight to live each and every day and of finding solace in Jesus ("Give Me Jesus") while relinquishing all concerns with the earthly world ("You Can Have All of This World But Give Me Jesus").

Du Bois speaks of three steps in the development of the slave songs: the first is African in origin, the second African American, and the third a blending of what he calls "Negro music" with that heard by those enslaved in their new homes, the "foster land."[9] The influence of European and Euro-American hymns has been shown in recent years, however, to be minimal. He also speaks of a possible fourth step, which today is recognized and honored, that of Black song influencing the development of the music of white ethnic America from Stephen Foster through the white jazz musicians of the nineteenth and twentieth centuries to Elvis Presley, the Beatles, and on to the emergence of the gospel music (Black and white) of today. Floyd affirms this but emphasizes the African and African American origins, noting that the spirituals were "created by American slaves as they participated in the process that Christianized them and as they performed their ring rituals, striving to retain their African memory."[10]

In two books, *The Negro's God as Reflected in His Literature* and *The Negro's Church*, Benjamin Mays presented the "development of the idea of God in Negro literature, 'mass' and 'classical,' from 1760 to 1937."[11] His understanding of "mass," or what today would be called popular religious literature, included the spirituals, sermons, prayers, and Sunday School literature. Like Du Bois, Mays also saw the spirituals as "one of the greatest contributions to American culture . . . a creation born of necessity in order that the slave might more adequately adjust himself to the new conditions in the new world." In his earlier work, *The Negro's Church*, he wrote:

> These songs are the expression of the restrictions and dominations which their creators experienced in the world about them. They represent the soul-life of the people. They embody the joy and sorrow, the hope and despair, the pathos and aspiration of the newly trans-planted people; and through them the race was able to endure suffering and survive. Clearly, the Negro spiritu-als are not songs of hate; they are not songs of revenge. They are songs neither of war nor of conquest. "They are songs of the soil and of the soul."[12]

Mays, like Du Bois, saw the spirituals in the sense of "sor-row songs," that is, "the traditional compensatory pattern" that was prevalent in the period between the Civil War/Recon-struction and the Civil Rights movement. This was a time of quietude or "passivity" on the part of many Blacks, especially in the Deep South, whose dream of freedom achieved was abruptly cut short by Reconstruction's politically constructed end in 1877. Thus, both men interpreted the songs from within their own contemporary perspective, a conservative one, and did not attempt to explore the beginnings of these songs and their emergence in slavery.

This "compensatory" understanding of God is described by Mays in this way:

> They are traditional in the sense that they are mainly those of orthodox Christianity as set forth in the Bible, with primary emphasis upon the magical, spectacular, partial, revengeful, and anthropomorphic nature of God

as revealed in the Old Testament; the New Testament ideas of a just, imported God; and those ideas of God that are being rapidly discarded in an age of science. The ideas are compensatory when used or developed to support a shallow pragmatism. That is, a belief or idea may be accredited as truth if it satisfies our desire; if it uplifts and consoles; or if it makes us "happier to believe it" even though the belief or idea does not fit observed facts.[13]

Although Mays recognizes and discusses a "constructive" idea of God "to support a growing consciousness of needed social adjustment," he and other Black religious scholars of the time (early to mid-twentieth century) were apparently unaware of the social consciousness and revolutionary ferment that permeated the spirituals from their earliest beginnings. This is due in part to the ignorance of the role these songs played in efforts toward liberation by the slaves. It is only with the increased interest of emerging Black theologians of the 1970s in the history of slavery, a history Blacks had shunned until that time, that this rich history has been uncovered and restored to us. Even the spirituals themselves were in danger of disappearing as Blacks refused to sing and/ or share them because of the painful memories they evoked.

The perspective of God that Mays articulates is, however, the first comprehensive effort to reveal the spiritual and theological thought of those enslaved in the United States for so many centuries. He notes that during this period Blacks felt that:

- God is omnipotent, omnipresent, and omniscient;
- God is sovereign, on heaven and on earth;
- God is just, sinners will be punished;
- God is revengeful;
- God is a warrior and fights the battles of his chosen people;

- God promises rest in heaven after death for those who hold out to the end;
- God is near and ever-present;
- God answers prayer.[14]

The spirituals, Mays asserts, fit a "compensatory" pattern because "they are ideas that enable Negroes to endure hardship, suffer pain, and withstand maladjustment." He argues that the spirituals" do not necessarily motivate them to strive to eliminate the source of the ills they suffer." He designates them as "otherworldly" and accepting of suffering leading to the "Negro" masses being inclined "to do little or nothing to improve their status here; they have been encouraged to rely on a *just* God to make amends for all the wrongs that they have suffered on the earth."[15] However, in light of contemporary knowledge, this statement is no longer regarded as true.

The understandings of the spirituals of Mays and Du Bois are accurate only in part, for, as Gayraud Wilmore has noted in speaking about Black history and theology, the spirituals, like the people who created and sang them, were holistic. Their songs were both compensatory and revolutionary, sometimes in the very same song.

Wilmore speaks of a pattern that can be traced to the beginnings of Blacks in the Americas, one that waxed and waned but presented a pattern of revolutionary fervor against their plight and passive—albeit not unchallenged—acceptance of their situation:

These two divergent tendencies in black ethics and religious life—the first tending toward radicalism, the other toward hypocritical compromise—represent two strands of a survival tradition. These strands of religion belong to what Lawrence W. Levine differentiated from traditional Christianity and called the slaves' "instruments of life, of sanity, of health, and of self-respect."[16]

The spirituals sung during the time of slavery were not just sorrow songs, singing about a faraway heavenly home. As researchers in the late 1960s and later realized from the ex-slave narratives that were retrieved from dusty storage—the vast witness of the former slaves compiled during the early 1930s by the Works Progress Administration—these songs were, in actuality, subversive, both in intent and in practice. James H. Cone was one of the first Black theologians to recognize and recover the true and often revolutionary meaning of the spirituals. As he affirms, rather than passive songs of tortured souls acquiescing in their hopeless fate while longing for their heavenly reward, the spirituals were theological texts that laid the groundwork for escape plans, rebellions, and other forms of resistance to their enslavement.

In his groundbreaking work *The Spirituals and the Blues*, Cone discusses the significance of Black music, of which the spirituals are the foremost example: "To interpret the theological significance of [a] spiritual for the black community, 'academic' tools are not enough. The interpreter must *feel* the Spirit; that is, one must feel one's way into the power of black music, responding both to its rhythm and the faith in experience it affirms."[17]

He uses the example of the spiritual "Every Time I Feel the Spirit" as the foundation for his statements:

> Every time I feel the spirit
> Moving in my heart I will pray.
> Every time I feel the spirit
> Moving in my heart I will pray.
>
> Upon the mountain my Lord spoke
> Out of his mouth came fire and smoke.
> In the valley on my knees,
> Asked my Lord, Have mercy, please.
>
> Every time I feel the spirit
> Moving in my heart I will pray.

Cone affirms that this song "invites the believer to move close to the very sources of black being, and to experience the black community's power to endure and the will to survive." He continues:

> The mountains may be high and the valleys low, but "my Lord spoke" and "out of his mouth came fire and smoke." All the believer has to do is to respond to the divine apocalyptic disclosure of God's revelation and cry, "Have mercy, please." This cry is not a cry of passivity, but a faithful, free response to the movement of God's Spirit. It is the Black community accepting themselves as the people of the Spirit and knowing through that presence that no chains can hold the spirit of Black humanity in bondage.[18]

For Cone, Black music, including the spirituals, is unity music in that it "shapes and defines black existence and creates cultural structures for black expression. Black music . . . confronts the individual with the truth of black existence and affirms that black being is possible only in a communal context." Black music is also functional as its purposes and aims "are directly related to the consciousness of the black community." It is a natural part of life. Cone also affirms that Black music is a living reality and is also social and political, serving as a rejection of white cultural values. Finally, it is also theological: "It tells us about the divine Spirit that moves the people toward unity and self-determination."[19]

It is also music about freedom. These songs reveal more than just a simple religious faith; they go far beyond ordinary religious boundaries as the singer daily, as the spiritual says, "woke up with my mind set on freedom." Floyd describes the spirituals as

> folk songs of freedom and faith in the inevitability of freedom. They are quasi-religious songs of longing and aspiration as well as chronicles of the black

slave experience in America—documents of impeccable truth and reliability—for they record the transition of the slave from African to African American, from slave to freedman, and the experiences that the African underwent in the transition.[20]

Social Consciousness

Songs such as "Steal Away," often sung at the request of masters who had no understanding of its true meaning, is believed to have been composed by Nat Turner, leader of a rebellion in 1831, as a means of communicating the time for meetings to discuss plans. It was also used by Harriet Tubman as a means of alerting the slaves to her presence in the surrounding woods and her plans to lead a group of slaves to freedom.

> Steal away, steal away,
> Steal away to Jesus.
> Steal away,
> Steal away home,
> I ain't got long to stay here.

Other songs, such as "Follow the Drinking Gourd," describe a route to freedom not in some far-off Canaan-land after death but in a very real and present route in the northern United States and in Canada. These songs, and many like them, reveal the complexity of African American spirituality, a spirituality that somehow flourished in conditions seemingly conducive only to despair and death. This spirituality was linked directly to the slaves' African ancestry but also borrowed heavily from the Christian beliefs to which they had been exposed, resulting in a syncretistic mix of African and Western worldviews that led to the emergence of something very new and very different. John Lovell saw the spiritual as "essentially social," and thus he examined the songs with regard to the social consciousness of those enslaved.[21]

According to Lovell, the social mind of the slaves "was a reflection of their African background, their life on southern plantations, and their encounter with their slave masters, overseers, auctioneers, and buyers. The songs were a reflection of this existence, and of the measures used to deal with the dehumanization inherent in it." Lovell affirmed that the spirituals were "the slave's description and criticism of his environment" and "the key to his revolutionary sentiments and to his desire to fly to free territory."[22] He found three distinct themes in the spirituals: "(1) a desire for freedom; (2) a 'desire for justice in the judgment of his betrayers'; and (3) 'a tactic battle, the strategy by which the slave expected to gain an eminent future.'"[23]

Singing their faith can be seen as an act of rebellion on the part of the slaves who "stole away" and "waded in the waters" to hush arbors, caves, hidden valleys, and other secret places in order to worship God in a style and manner that brought peace to their souls. In these songs, we see the first linkings of a demand for social justice with a theology that proclaimed they too were created in God's own image and likeness. In their hidden places their denial of the right of their masters to hold them against their will and to treat them as beasts of burden was clearly brought out, as they sang

> Freedom, freedom
> Freedom over me
> And before I'll be a slave
> I'll be buried in my grave
> And go home to my Lord and be free.

This song clearly reveals their resistance to what they were taught was their God-appointed state in life, while the one below reveals how they saw their situation. It is said that "Go

Down, Moses" was first sung at a hush arbor service after
Nat Turner was captured.

> Go down, Moses
> Way down in Egypt land.
> Tell old Pharaoh
> To let my people go.

They took their burden to God, and they believed God
would respond, albeit in God's own time. Perhaps that response was not as quick and decisive as they would have liked
but they understood, as the spiritual says, "He may not come
when you want him but he's always right on time." Again,
theirs was a spirituality of resistance, a resistance forged in
the smelting pot of slavery, plantation life, auctions, and
rebellions against the lie that their very existence denied. In
other words, the slaves did not feel alone or abandoned by
God. Although they sang of loss of friends, family, and community, they held to their holistic understanding of God's
ability to overcome all things:

> Sometimes I feel like a motherless child,
> Sometimes I feel like a motherless child,
> Sometimes I feel like a motherless child,
>   a long way from home.

After mourning the loss of all that enables one to survive, they
were able to sing of a joy that contradicted the sorrow. The
song ends in an affirmation of ongoing faith:

> True believer! True believer!
> A long way from home

The slaves were not naive or in any way childish. They
understood their situation for what it was, a living death,
but they attempted to counter that death by maintaining a

spiritual life that enabled them to continue rather than giving up in despair. They sang, "Lord, how come me here? I wish I'd never been born," but they also sang, "My soul looks back and wonders how I got over"—how they got over the dehumanization, the depravity, the deprivation that made up so much of their everyday life. They "got over" because of their fathomless faith in a God of action who sent his Son with a promise of salvation for all, not just some of humanity. They "got over" because of their belief in a "wonderworking God" who did not like "ugly" and would, in God's time, bring about their liberation, not solely in death, but in their physical life as well. They "got over" because they knew that the Holy Spirit could undo anything that humanity attempted to do. In the words of St. Anselm, they were a people of faith seeking understanding of that faith. In crafting their songs of love, of sorrow, of haunting grief, and of unvanquishable hope, they created the first African American theology. The minor chords and often dragging melodies seemed to speak only of hopelessness and despair but in actuality were the "masks" that hid the true and rebellious faith of a people others still condemn to the lower ranks of humanity. In their songs they revealed knowledge of the reality of the United States that still is not fully revealed anywhere else to this day.

Rechristianizing Christianity

In their lives of faith they forged a new Christianity, one that negated the distortions of the Christianity foisted upon them by white Christians. Denying the legality of their slavery, they formulated an ethical perspective very different from that taught them, one that "reflected the requirements of *black* existence. Right and wrong were determined by *survival* needs in the context of servitude."[24] For example, they distinguished between "stealing" and "taking"; taking applied to the property or belongings of whites, which were rightfully their property as they had built, planted, hoed, picked, and made it of value; stealing, however, was seen as a sin because it meant "victimizing" a brother or sister slave.

> Slaves were able to live a different ethical style than their masters because they constructed a different religion. . . . Religion is not a set of beliefs that people memorize and neither is it an ethical code of do's and don'ts that they learn from others. Rather religion is wrought out of the experience of the people who encounter the divine in the midst of historical realities.[25]

The spirituals reveal this reborn Christianity, this rechristianized Christianity, for they are the essence of Black religion and Black spirituality. They are directly and intimately related to daily life, work, and play, thereby revealing their connection all the way back to Africa:

> African culture provided the form that made it impossible for Black slaves to accept a religion that negated their being as defined by their African heritage. In the spirituals, Black slaves combined the memory of their fathers [and mothers] with the Christian gospel and created a style of existence that participated in their liberation from earthly bondage.[26]

In their efforts to understand their situation and their faith, those enslaved and those who came after them claimed their foster land as their homeland, one for which they had fought, sweat, bled, and died over the several centuries of the formation of this new country, the United States of America. Du Bois articulated their assertion of their ownership and citizenship forcefully:

> Your country? How came it yours? Before the Pilgrims landed we were here. Here we have brought our three gifts and mingled them with yours: a gift of story and

song—soft, stirring melody in an ill-harmonized and unmelodious land; the gift of sweat and brawn to beat back the wilderness, conquer the soil, and lay the foundations of this vast economic empire two hundred years earlier than your weak hands could have done it; the third, a gift of the Spirit. Around us the history of the land has centered for thrice a hundred years; out of the nation's heart we have called all that was best to throttle and subdue all that was worst; fire and blood, prayer and sacrifice, have billowed over this people, and they have found peace only in the altars of the God of Right. Nor has our gift of the Spirit been merely passive. Actively we have woven ourselves with the very warp and woof of this nation,—we fought their battles, shared their sorrow, mingled our blood with theirs, and generation after generation have pleaded with a headstrong, careless people to despise not Justice, Mercy, and Truth, lest the nation be smitten with a curse. Our song, our toil, our cheer, and warning have been given this nation in blood-brotherhood. . . . Would America have been America without her Negro people?[27]

Post–Civil War/Post-Reconstruction

For a brief period after the Civil War these songs were threatened with oblivion as the freed slaves, who wanted nothing that would remind them of their shame-filled pasts, looked ahead to a brighter future. James Weldon Johnson and J. Rosamund Johnson have described this time as follows:

These songs passed through a period when the front ranks of the Negro race would have been willing to let them die. Immediately following Emancipation those ranks revolted against everything connected with slavery, and among those things were the Spirituals. It became a sign of not being progressive or educated to sing them.

. . . It was left for the older generation to keep them alive by singing them at prayer meetings, class meetings, experience meetings and revivals, while the new choir with the organ and books of idiotic anthems held sway on Sunday.[28]

The few achievements Blacks had made after the Civil War and the end of slavery were quickly reversed. After 1877 the white South, with the rest of the United States as silent accomplices, harshly and firmly relegated former slaves to the pseudo-slave status of feudal sharecroppers, binding them to land they did not own with few rewards and little hope of achieving land or any other form of independence of their own.[29]

The short-lived Reconstruction period, the end of which found them once more captives of the land and the land's owners, helped them, however, to realize that the days of sorrow had not passed. In small churches and large, the music and words of the spirituals still served to heal their wounded souls and ease their troubled minds. The spirituals were revived, often with the same melody but new words, to fit their contemporary situation. I believe that it is from this time period that we can trace the meaning and intention of the spirituals as the means for a re-enslaved people to deal with their crushed hopes of freedom.

This period also saw the revival of the old songs, rewritten and performed in more classical styles, by college choirs, especially the Fisk Jubilee Singers of Fisk University. Traveling through the United States and Europe to raise funds for their school, they discovered that there was more interest in hearing them sing the spirituals than in hearing them sing European melodies. Both traditions persist to this day, on and off campus and in and out of churches.

It was through the spirituals that the slaves made the Christian religion their own and "reaffirmed their traditional world-view (modified by the realities of slavery and the myths and rituals of Christian religion)."[30] It was through their music and prayers that they built a community of faith that enabled them to survive and move forward. The spirituals and hush/brush arbors were the framework for what later became the Black church. Although they are still sung, they also gave birth to a more contemporary form of religious music, gospel music, which also comes from the heart of the Black community, providing Black people in modern times a place of quiet refuge as well as a stimulant for action.

5

Oh, Freedom!

The Emergence of the Black Church

Oh, Freedom, oh, Freedom
Oh, freedom over me
And before I'd be a slave
I'd be buried in my grave
And go home to my Lord and be free
—Negro Spiritual

Freedom's Beginning: Slavery's End

When freedom came at the end of the Civil War, those formerly enslaved realized that their lives had irrevocably changed. They credited that change to the grace and will of a loving God and Savior, who had fulfilled the promises made them during the long, horrible years of slavery in the United States. These promises had been made, not by those who had enslaved them, but had been passed on by those fellow Christians, themselves often still slaves, who had been raised up in their communities as preachers and exhorters. Their fiery and fervent proclamation of the word of God revealed the true meaning of the message of Jesus Christ for them. That message was one of liberation, of humans made in the image and likeness of God who were called to persevere in their captivity until the Lord made a way for them out of the wilderness.

89

Their faith bolstered their spirits and encouraged them to challenge the status quo, as numerous rebellions revealed.

According to Albert Raboteau, the slave exhorters of the late eighteenth and early nineteenth century "acted as crucial mediators between Christian beliefs and the experiential world of the slaves. In effect, they were helping to shape the development of a bi-cultural synthesis, in Afro-American culture, by nurturing the birth of Christian communities among blacks, slave and free."[1]

The aftermath of the First and Second Awakenings, as already discussed, saw the opening of the doors of Christian churches to those enslaved and those already free, setting forth a movement that continues to the present day, the establishing of churches, small and large, both within predominantly white denominations and increasingly in independent freestanding churches of their own. The freedom to worship meant that the slaves found, especially in the Methodist and Baptist denominations, a sense of place and openness to the Spirit that spoke to their self-understanding and their religious sensibilities. It enabled them to develop a religious faith that was authentically Black and rooted in their African worldview *and* their experiences in the Americas. Black religion continued to serve as a source of comfort, refuge, and challenge for them, as Gayraud Wilmore affirms, noting that

> for the slaves and their descendants, a religion that could unveil the reality of another world beyond "this vale of tears" and at the same time interpret what God was doing to redress the wrongs against blacks was an absolute necessity for survival. . . . It was precisely the mystique and so-called other worldliness of black religion that gave it license to speak authoritatively about daily life, about oppression and liberation. "Going to church" . . . was a necessity. The church was the one impregnable corner of the world where consolation, unity, and mutual assistance could be found and from which the master—at least in the North—could be

effectively barred if the people were not of a mind to welcome him.[2]

As indicated in Chapter 3, their resistance to the teachings of white masters and preachers of a passive Christianity enabled them to withstand efforts to strip them of their humanity and dignity. They fought against these teachings by using the stories and sayings of the Bible as a weapon to reveal and attack the distorted Christianity foisted upon them.

This is why during the period of slavery whites sought with every means available to them to curb the proclamation of the gospel to Blacks; they especially did not want it proclaimed by Blacks themselves, except under strictly controlled circumstances. This is also why Blacks believed that "the gospel must have something very important to do with the freedom and well-being of blacks."[3] Buoyed up by the spirit of their ancestors, they dug deep within themselves to forge a link between the African spirituality of their past and the African American spirituality that was coming to birth. It was "African spirituality [that] helped those forced into slavery redefine themselves, find unity, and express inner strength, despite the experience of oppression. Further, African spirituality buffered white slave owners' attempts to destroy African cultural identity."[4]

Once freedom came, or so they thought, Blacks fought to sustain and retain the faith that had enabled them to persevere. The "invisible institution" of slave religion had to reformulate itself in many ways to appeal to those formerly enslaved as well as to those who had been free for generations. Black religion, "characterized by its theological diversity and its broad spectrum of cultural nuances,"[5] had to restructure itself, opening itself up to new realities, while at the same time retaining much if not all of what was viable from the period of slavery. Shawn Copeland speaks to the essence of Black religion in asserting that it is a "historical phenomenon *neither* Protestant *nor* Catholic, normatively centered in an African worldview, even if the language of its expression and the symbols of its ritual are Christian in inspiration and, in fact, *even* if the very features of the Christianity peculiar to the enslaved peoples masked their Africanity."[6]

The religious expression that developed over the centuries-long span of slavery and continued after slavery's end took different forms in different places, as we have already seen, depending on differing societal and cultural values as well as social status (free or enslaved), economic status (poor or middle class), and location (urban or rural). However, all Black religious expression contains most if not all of the following attributes. It is animistic, anthropocentric, dynamic, expressionistic, historic, messianic, nationalistic, shamanistic, and thaumaturgic (belief in miracle working).[7]

It thus bears repeating that the Christianity of those enslaved and newly freed was very different from the religion of those who had attempted to impose a distorted vision of faith upon them. Black Christians' belief system may have been structurally similar to that of whites but it had a very different theological emphasis, as Leonard Gadzekpo explains in his discussion of the Black church:

> The major aspect of black Christian belief was embodied in the word "freedom." Freedom for whites encompassed the value of American individualism, freedom to "pursue one's destiny without political or bureaucratic interference or restraint." For the African in America as a slave, it meant release from bondage; after emancipation, it meant education, employment, and freedom of movement to the "Negro"; . . . At the same time, freedom to African Americans through the centuries was also communal in nature.[8]

The most "critical aspect" of the African American understanding of freedom was its definition as "the absence of any restraint which might compromise one's responsibility to God." Having lived for generations in environments hostile to their unique expression of the Christian faith, African Americans were determined to "joy their freedom" now that it had finally come. For them, "a call to God's discipleship was a call to freedom" because "the Christian doctrine provided the legitimate ethical foundation that related equality directly to God's creative activities."[9]

It is this emphasis on freedom that led Blacks, enslaved and free, to develop their own churches in which they could worship in a style and manner that suited their African natures and spirituality. These churches were both freestanding and dependent on white denominations, but their most critical aspect was that Blacks sought to control, as best they could, their spiritual and worship lives, despite the resistance of others.

Freedom's Spirit: The Black Church

Origins

The Black church was "born in protest, tested in adversity, led by eloquent and courageous preachers. . . . [It] was the cutting edge of the freedom movement during most of the nineteenth century."[10] The Black church had its beginnings in slavery while its roots are in Africa. Efforts by Blacks to understand the horrible new circumstances in which they found themselves in the Americas led them to reassert their indigenous religious beliefs while, at the same time, they were drawn to the new beliefs surrounding them on the plantations and farms and in the homes in which they found themselves captives. As previously discussed, they did not simply accept the Christian faith as handed to them or forced upon them by their overseers but went beyond the superficial to the core of Christianity's affirmation of the freedom and equality of all human beings based on their creation by God the eternal Father. As Raboteau affirms, the "slaves did not simply become Christians; they creatively fashioned a Christian tradition to fit their own freedom experience of enslavement in America."[11]

Their efforts led to the "invisible institution" exemplified in hush arbors and brush arbors tucked away in many areas, North and South, but it also led, especially after the Second Great Awakening, to the emergence of true religious institutions. These first churches that emerged in the South in the late 1700s were led by Blacks and their congregations were entirely Black. Churches like Silver Bluff in South Carolina (founded sometime between 1773 and 1775), considered the mother church of many Baptist missions in the South, and other small churches prospered until they were forcibly shut down by whites who were afraid of the possible consequences of allowing Blacks to congregate freely. This became especially important after several rebellions and insurrections were led by faith-filled slaves who sought to live out their faith in a liberating God. By the 1820s most Southern Black churches "were supervised by whites, ending the early freedoms of Blacks in raising churches and choosing pastors."[12] Most were integrated as well with Blacks having a subordinate role and little participation in church activities.

The Black church has been defined in a number of different ways in an effort to encompass the depth and breadth of the unique community that African peoples were able to develop under torturous conditions in the United States of America. The term *Black church* leads back into the history of the people of African descent and stretches in a nearly unbroken line of resistance to slavery and dehumanization back to the first Africans brought to the Americas and grudgingly, often cynically, introduced to a form of Christianity that sought to demonstrate their fitness for slavery. In *Black Church Studies*, Stacey Floyd-Thomas points out the form and function of the church, noting that

> The Black Church emerges from the religious, cultural, and social experience of Black people. With its roots

on the continent of Africa and the Middle Passage, the Black Church provided structure and meaning for African people and their descendants in the Americas who struggled to survive the ravages and brutality of slavery and racial oppression. . . . The Black Church functioned as the center of Black life, culture, and heritage for much of the history of the African American experience in North America.[13]

Prior to slavery's end the Black church existed as a structural entity in very few areas of the United States, mostly in the North, where Blacks had greater freedom to form institutions that were independent of white supervision. Yet its roots were very much present in the South in the "invisible institution," the hidden and often not-so-hidden places of worship founded by those enslaved who sought the freedom to worship in a style and manner that provided comfort and solace for their present state. As W. E. B. Du Bois observes:

In origin and functions the Negro church is a broader, deeper, and more comprehensive social organization than the churches of white America. The Negro church is not simply an organism for the propagation of religion; it is the centre of the social, intellectual, and religious life of an organized group of individuals. . . . It is, in fine, the central organism of the organized life of the American Negro for amusement, relaxation, instruction, and religion.[14]

The term *Negro church* was first introduced by W. E. B. Du Bois in the early part of the twentieth century:

The Negro church is the only social institution of the Negros that started in the African forest and survived slavery; under the leadership of priest or medical man, afterward of the Christian pastor, the Church preserved in itself the remnants of African tribal life and became after emancipation the center of Negro social life. So that today the Negro population of the United States is virtually divided into congregations which are the real units of race life.[15]

In other words, the Black community historically has been defined and is identifiable by means of its religious configuration, the various congregations and denominations that make it a solid voting bloc, a source of charitable endeavor, and a leader in providing education.

Du Bois speaks of the Black church as it is often depicted, as representing the Black Protestant churches that emerged in the South and North originally as part of or dependent upon white churches on plantations and in urban areas but that eventually became independent of them. However, the understanding today is much broader and includes those persons of African descent who were members of white denominations as well, such as the Anglican/Episcopal, Presbyterian, and Roman Catholic churches. The Black Catholic bishops of the United States have affirmed this in their pastoral letter "What We Have Seen and Heard":

There exists what is called "The Black church." It crosses denominational boundaries and is without a formal structure. Yet it is a reality cherished by many Black Christians, who feel at ease in joining in prayer and in Christian action with one another. This Black Church is a result of our common experience and history—it has made it possible for many Blacks to understand and appreciate each other.[16]

Leadership in the Black Church

Du Bois also discussed the continuity between the African priest and the African American priest, which led to the founding of the "Negro" church:

The vast power of the priest in the African state still survived; his realm alone—the province of religion and medicine—remained largely unaffected by the plantation system in many important particulars. The Negro priest, therefore, early became an important figure on the plantation and found his function as the interpreter of the supernatural, the comforter of the sorrowing, and as the one who expressed, rudely but picturesquely, the longing and disappointment and resentment of a stolen people. From such beginnings rose and spread with marvelous rapidity the Negro church, the first distinctively Negro American social institution. . . . After two centuries, the Church became Christian, with a simple Calvinistic creed, but with many of the old customs still clinging to the services. It is this historic fact that the Negro Church today bases itself upon the sole surviving social institution of the African fatherland, that accounts for its extraordinary growth and vitality.[17]

The role of the pastor as leader and spokesperson, representing the tribal leaders and/or shaman of Africa and performing similar roles, was critical to the formation of the Black church, just as the "African chieftain was responsible for the welfare of his people." He acted as protector, provider, and counselor while the shaman provided spiritual guidance and served as a liaison to the metaphysical realm.[18] Quite often, as in Africa, the chief and shaman were one and the same person.

Men, for the most part, both slave and free, recognized for their deep spirituality, their faith, as well as their speaking ability, their facility at extemporaneous prayer, and their lives of moral rectitude, quickly became leaders of those enslaved and those who were free.[19] They were selected by their fellow worshipers, although often this selection had to be ratified by white pastors or plantation owners. Many of them, however, recognized the ability of these men (and some few women) spiritually to serve their own and often white congregations as well.

Development of Independent Black Churches

The Methodist and Baptist churches were the most popular in both the South and the North. They split in the late eighteenth century over the issue of slavery, forming Northern (anti-slavery) and Southern (pro-slavery) branches with similar doctrines and practices except on the issue of slavery. Other churches—Presbyterian, Episcopal, and Roman Catholic—welcomed Blacks, slave and free, but did not separate or in any way change their style of worship or ritual to accommodate them. It is in the North that we see the fruition of the African American desire to have autonomy in religious life. Two independent denominations emerged, the African Methodist Episcopal Church (AME, 1787/1816) under the leadership and guidance of Richard Allen in Philadelphia, and the African Methodist Episcopal Zion Church (AMEZ, 1796/1820) under James Varick in New York. A third church (1794), the African Episcopal Church, later affiliated with the Protestant Episcopal Church under Absalom Jones.[20]

The AME and Episcopal churches were the result of the actions taken by free Blacks in response to the discriminatory treatment they received at St. George Methodist Church in Philadelphia. Restricted to the balcony and kept from kneeling to pray at the altar, the majority of Black members walked out and formed the Free African Society, a church in all but name. It was a charitable institution whose object was to provide for not only religious needs but also social services, mutual aid, and solidarity among those of African descent. This was in keeping with the African understanding that there is no separation between religious life and secular life, which are deeply and intimately intertwined. Gayraud Wilmore describes this form of institution as "a church without actually being one . . . a fellowship of black citizens who craved independence and social progress without reference to the creeds and confessions used in most mainline churches."[21]

The founding of the Free African Society served as a model or pattern for what became the future independent Black churches. It was "a pattern of religious commitment that has a double focus: free and autonomous worship in the Afro-American tradition and the solidarity and social welfare of the black community."[22]

The Black churches in the South reemerged and flourished in the period after the end of slavery as Blacks sought to maintain their freedom; find missing parents, children, and spouses; and the most prized freedom of all, learn to read and write. Ira Berlin writes of the continuity of meaning and message that the Black churches provided for the formerly enslaved Blacks.

> The black church remained—as it had been in slave times—the center of rural Black life. Its minister's message rarely veered from a close reading of the gospel and, in his official pronouncements, almost always steered away from anything that could be deemed offensive to the white planters and merchants whose shadows loomed over the lives of his congregants. The weekly sermons presented a stern but loving God who would balance the scales of justice and offered hope not only for the next world but also for the here and now; as He had promised, faith had delivered His people from slavery and it would deliver them from the current injustices. Meanwhile the weekly gatherings became the occasion for the believers—and not a few skeptics—to nourish their stomachs as well as their souls, bind themselves together as a community, recognize their frailties, gather their courage, and affirm their worth. The torrent of emotions renewed the faith of people who had little else but faith, reassuring them that they were God's children and that he had not forsaken them.[23]

The Black church movement can arguably be said to be the first freedom movement in Black history, especially "during and following the period of the Revolutionary War"; it was the prime expression of resistance to slavery and an act of rebellion against white American churches.[24] This was so because the churches in the North, especially, offered spaces where African Americans could confer and worship as they pleased, free of white surveillance. The Black church usually provided the only meeting space where Blacks could freely congregate and engage in political discussions without restraint. It was here, in their churches, that they found the freedom to express themselves, to protest harsh and unjust treatment, and to provide education for their children. All ages and genders found the church a place of spiritual uplift as well as day-to-day encouragement.

What Is the Black Church?

So what exactly is the Black church? That still remains to be seen because its definition is as varied and diverse as the people who make it up. One of the fullest definitions is that of Stacey Floyd-Thomas, who states that "the Black church consists of . . . those churches whose worship life and cultural sensibilities have reflected, historically and traditionally, a connection to the larger African American community." She notes three primary expressions:

- Independent Baptist, Methodist, and Holiness-Pentecostal denominations;
- Black congregations and fellowship in predominantly white denominations: Roman Catholic, Presbyterian, and Episcopalian; and
- In the latter part of the twentieth century, non-denominational Christian churches with multicultural, multiracial, and multiethnic membership but whose ministerial leadership and cultural identity are African American.[25]

Others, such as womanist Delores Williams, have developed a more dynamic understanding:

> The black church does not exist as an institution. Regardless of sociological, theological, historical and pastoral attempts, the black church escapes precise definition. . . . Some believe it to be rooted deeply in the soul of the community memory of black folk. Some believe it to be the core symbol of the four-hundred-year-old African American struggle against white oppression with God in the struggle providing black people with spiritual and material resources for survival and freedom. Others believe it to be places where black people come to worship God without white people being present.
>
> I believe the black church is the heart of hope in the black community's experience of oppression, survival struggle and its historic efforts toward complete liberation.[26]

Williams distinguishes between the Black church as a spiritual entity unbounded and limitless and the particular African American denominational congregations. Not to do so would, in her opinion, imply a unity that does not exist.[27] It would also, she believes, cover up the many sins the denominational churches have committed against women who, although considered the "backbone" of the Black church, have too often been denied full equality within them.

The Black church in this perspective is invisible, residing in the hearts, minds, and spirits of Black folk. As Barbara Holmes explains, the Black church has "an actual and meta-actual form [that] inhabits the imagination of its people in ways that far exceed its reach. . . . It embodies a spiritual idea. This idea is grounded not only in history but also in the narratives and myths of an oppressed people. The black church [is] a spiritual wellspring."[28]

Freedom's Betrayal: The Rise of Jim Crow

Freedom was short lived. The first phase of what could be called Presidential Reconstruction lasted only a year, from 1865 to 1866, and was more beneficial to the Confederate states and their citizens than to the newly freed slaves. The Federal Government promised freedom in the form of forty acres and a mule (General Sherman) to each freed person or family, to be funded by the confiscated land and property of the rebels. However, President Andrew Johnson began the process of reinstating both the citizenship and property of the Confederates through pardons and oaths of allegiance almost immediately, leaving little land to be distributed. In actuality, only about two thousand persons out of millions of former slaves actually received land and were able to keep it. The rest were quickly forced into sharecropping and other roles that were very similar to their situation before the war's end but that lacked the few protections that had then existed.[29]

The majority of Blacks in the South had no desire to leave but sought to find means of supporting themselves and reuniting with family members who had been sold off or forcibly moved away by their owners before the war. Their major goals were to have homes and land of their own and, equally important, to become literate.

The second phase of Reconstruction can be designated Congressional or radical because the U.S. Congress took over the responsibility for those formerly enslaved. It is here that we see what could have been in terms of Blacks being accepted into mainstream American life. In the period from 1867 to 1877, Congress passed amendments to the U.S. Constitution that stipulated that the basic human and civil rights applicable to all Americans also applied to Blacks, or at least to those who were male. These amendments, the Thirteenth, Fourteenth, and Fifteenth, confirmed that slavery was illegal and that Blacks born in the United States, like all others so born, were citizens of the United States of America with the right to vote (males only) and to lead their lives as they wished.

As a result, Black men were able to vote and stand for office in the South for the first time in U.S. history. They did so in large numbers. The great majority of those who did, although not all, were pastors and other religious leaders who had managed to acquire literacy, most often by reading the Bible, and who saw themselves as speaking for the great mass of freed men and women. Men like Henry Highland Garnett, Henry McNeal Turner, Hiram Revels, and others spoke eloquently of the needs and concerns of the millions of freed persons who were seeking their way in this challenging and hope-filled new era.

That hope was pressed down but not completely extinguished even when Congressional Reconstruction was abruptly ended by the election of President Rutherford B. Hayes in a scandal-riven election in 1876. All federal troops and therefore all protection for those who had opposed slavery were hastily removed, leaving the freed men and women to the indignities, hatreds, and prejudices of their former owners. The result was the era of Jim Crow, a form of slavery in all but name, in which Blacks were forced into menial labor such as sharecropping, were stripped of their civil rights and of their human dignity, and were stigmatized and degraded by whites with impunity.[30] Very similar in tone, restrictions, and intention to the Black Codes of the antebellum South, Jim Crow simply refined and intensified the Code in the South and was copied in many other parts of the United States. As Nell Painter notes, it was a rigid system of racial apartheid:

> A formidable structure of Jim Crow laws grew up in the South . . . and erected new barriers of segregation and discrimination on trains, streetcars, steamboats, and in almost every other area of interracial contact. States and local communities passed legislation prohibiting the races from working together in the same room, using the same entrances, stairways, drinking water, and toilets.

Blacks were excluded from public institutions such as theaters, amusement parks, and residential neighborhoods. . . . Jim Crow Bibles were . . . used for Black witnesses in the Atlanta courts.[31]

The freed men and women did not give up their struggle, however. During Reconstruction, numerous Black schools were opened at every level from elementary to college with courses for adults in the evenings. Blacks continued to fight for the right to learn how to read and write. Painter describes the situation of former slaves at this time:

Black achievement in the South during the era of Reconstruction was enormous. But every success occurred against a backdrop of intimidation and actual bloodshed. African Americans reconstructed their families, pursued formal education and created their own institutions. Men tried to vote and hold office as though they lived in a democracy. They did not. For black people, democracy proved limited and fleeting. However, the institutions created during the larger era of Reconstruction (1864–96) endured.[32]

The Black Church: Post-Reconstruction

One of the greatest sources of support for the freed slaves was the growing number of independent Black churches. The church was the only place where they could safely and freely express their sorrow and their joy, their unvanquished hope in a God greater not only than themselves but also than those who oppressed them. It was usually a small, whitewashed wooden structure tucked away in the woods to which they flocked on Sundays and, if possible, other days of the week as well to hear about and rejoice in a "wonderworking God" whose hand they believed was still over, around, and on them, blessing and guiding them on their way.

The Protestant churches, especially Methodist and Baptist, expanded rapidly after the Civil War. Many of those who had been members of the Southern Methodist Church left in droves to form the Colored Methodist Episcopal Church (after 1965 it became the Christian Methodist Episcopal Church), while those in Southern Baptist, Presbyterian, and Episcopal Churches formed their own congregations and or denominations.[33]

This recourse was not as available to Black Catholics, and many left the Catholic Church not because of a failure of faith but due to a failure of courage on the part of the American bishops. Encouraged by the Vatican to establish a special vicariate (or diocese) for those newly freed, they instead chose to do nothing. Even though the Vatican condemned slavery, the Catholic Church in the United States did little to oppose it and even supported it within its episcopal and religious institutions, where slaves served many, from bishops, religious sisters, brothers, and priests, down to the lowest layperson who had the funds to purchase a fellow Christian human being. One of the largest such entities prior to the Civil War was the Jesuits, who maintained numerous tobacco plantations in Maryland to support their ministry, which included the founding of the first Jesuit institution of higher learning, Georgetown University.[34]

The newly freed Catholics resisted the restrictions placed on them when worshiping in white spaces and often demanded their own church buildings and schools, taught by African American sisters such as those of the Oblate Sisters of Providence or the Holy Family, two Black women's religious congregations. Even then, however, they had to share a white priest with the white parishioners.

Resistance to white efforts to re-enslave them in all but name was the key for both Catholic and Protestant Black Christians, but differences multiplied within the Black community as to what form that resistance should take. Early religious leaders vehemently protested the re-enslavement of their people and fought against it. One such was Henry

McNeal Turner (1834–1915), a vocal bishop in the AME Church who was elected to political office in South Carolina during Reconstruction. Confronted by what he saw as the growing passivity of the Black church, Turner fought vigorously for Black elevation, but in a very different style and manner than did Booker T. Washington (1856–1915), who, after the death of Frederick Douglass (1818–95), became the recognized leader of African Americans. Turner was of the "old school" of fiery and politically engaged preachers who argued for reparations for slavery and proclaimed that "God is a Negro" to support his denunciation of white Christianity. As W. E. B. Du Bois affirmed, "Turner was the last of his clan: mighty men, physically and mentally, men who started at the bottom and hammered their way to the top by sheer brute strength; they were the spiritual progeny of ancient African chieftains and they built the African church in America."[35] His was a spirituality of resolute resistance, as opposed to the more passive spirit of survival that became more common in the Black church.

Freedom Deferred: An Alternate Spirituality

Although Black resistance was consistent, it became increasingly moderate in the late nineteenth and early twentieth centuries. Booker T. Washington's gradualism became "adopted by most Black preachers not only because they lacked the courage to fight back but because it was consonant with the ethics of the white Christianity by which they were increasingly influenced."[36]

The picture of the nonviolent, self-effacing, patiently suffering white Jesus held up by the conservative evangelicals and revivalists at the turn of the century became for many Black preachers the authoritative image of what it is like to be a Christian. The image provided irrefutable confirmation, supported by scripture, of the wisdom and expediency of Washington's position.[37]

Although there were numerous opponents to Booker T. Washington's accommodationism, they were not usually Black preachers, most of who were firmly ensconced by the twentieth century as members of the new Black bourgeoisie and saw little reason to rattle the cages. Wilmore notes, "They did not have the common touch . . . and they regarded civil rights agitation more as a last resort for breaking into the American mainstream than as a means of precipitating a crisis that would confront the basic assumptions of the system and create a feeling of nationalism among the masses."[38] It is indeed ironic that a church birthed in the violence of slavery would now accept passively the Christianity that its founding members, those who had been enslaved, had fought so vigorously against.

It must, however, be recognized that, having acquired a freedom of sorts at least religiously if not politically and economically, twentieth-century Blacks sought to preserve what they had gained rather than risk its destruction by the forces they knew continued to exist but were temporarily held at bay. Their conservatism was not due to apathy or low morale but to a strong sense of self-preservation. They turned inward, nurturing a spirituality that still sang of freedom but more and more a freedom away from this world of prejudice and discrimination. Theirs became a "pie in the sky when you die" spirituality, an "otherworldly" faith that fostered a form of escapism that persists to the present day. That does not mean the revolutionary spirituality of their ancestors was completely lost; it still persisted, simmering quietly deep within them and waiting for the time when it could once more burst forth in bold, vigorous, and renewed resistance.

Gayraud Wilmore refers to this persistent tension with the Black community and especially the Black churches when he writes of a "dark and contrary side" of Black religion, one that must be understood as an "alternative form of spirituality. It is a fundamental aspect of what we may call the survival tradition." He continues:

It has been indelibly imprinted on a persistently hetero-
dox form of Christianity that has come down through
black churches and cults into this century. Although
it was often expressed as a curiously divergent form
of spirituality, it is not to be equated with the kind of
pietism that can be transformed into social reform. It
often had, rather, a bitter unsentimentality about it. It
was more often cynical, manipulative, and, at the very
least, ambivalent about spiritual things.[39]

This alternative spirituality was the source of new forms
of music, the secular songs and blues that emerged in the
early twentieth century along with jazz.[40] The music was
both ironic and tragic in voice, making fun of traditional
religion while remaining steeped in its mores and ideology. It
was a response to lives of hard work, poverty, and despair as
Blacks continued to resist the white supremacy that constantly
threatened to invade and take over their neighborhoods,
families, and lives. Wilmore sees this as a polar opposite to
the more radical religious life that had historically existed in
Black America. He speaks, as noted earlier, of "two divergent
tendencies in Black ethics and religious life—the first tending
toward radicalism, the other toward hypocritical compromise"—that represent two strands of a survival tradition.[41]

Du Bois saw this survival religion as a search for a "new
religious ideal." He recognized that what the white evangelical churches had passed on to Blacks had been thoroughly
adulterated by the end of slavery, merged with a subterranean
stream of African spirituality and the survival instincts of an
impoverished and downtrodden people. In this condition, he
wrote, "broods silently the deep religious feeling of the real
Negro heart, the stirring, unguided might of powerful human
souls who have lost the guiding star of the past and seek in
the great night a new religious ideal."[42]

Throughout, the Black pastors remained as the leaders of
their people. They were involved in the Niagara Movement,
which led to the founding of the National Association for

the Advancement of Colored People (NAACP, 1909), and in other civil, social, and political activities, exhorting their followers to hold on for a better tomorrow while presenting a face of compromise to the powers that be. Many churches were burned, especially in the South, and many Blacks were lynched for daring to speak about freedom and God's hatred of Jim Crow. But Blacks persisted in their belief that God would prevail and that, someday soon, they would truly be free, not just spiritually but, more important, socially and economically.

The radically liberating ethos of the Black church was not gone, but the church had indeed "hunkered down" in a protective, survival stance in order to ensure the safety of the lives of its faithful congregants. They persisted in their belief that God was a God of liberation, of freedom; that Blacks were meant to be free, not slaves; and that Blacks were human beings, not animals, and were therefore worthy of dignity and respect from all. For them, the Black church was home, a place of safety, where all needs were satisfied and all fears abated. As E. U. Essien-Udom asserts:

> The church gave the black person pride in success, grassroots participation in a national movement, independence from white control, and a physical center for social life in the black community. . . . The black church, as the primary institutional expression of black religion, created the politico-theological foundation for black nationalism and Pan-Africanism. Not only did it provide the organizational skills requisite for mass movements in the 20th century, it provided also the spiritual inspiration and theological rationale—building blocks for the structure of African and Afro-American solidarity as it developed from the early Du Bois to Malcolm X.[43]

6

My Soul Is Rested

The Struggle for Justice

"My feets is tired, but my soul is rested."
—MOTHER POLLARD[1]

"A Change Is Gonna' Come"[2]

The period between 1955 and 1968 saw what can only be called the fruition of the spiritual and physical struggle of the African American people. They had toiled and labored, struggled and climbed, and kept their faith alive for over four hundred years in the face of all obstacles. God could be seen, once again, to be acting in their lives as they fervently believed God had done throughout their sojourn in the United States, but especially at slavery's end after the Civil War. Once again God was clearly on their side as the hated Jim Crow laws and their dehumanizing restrictions began to tumble and fall. African Americans were stepping out on their faith and not allowing anything or anyone to turn them around. And, as during slavery, God sent men and women to help them walk forth into freedom. They were preachers and teachers, adults and children, ordinary men and women who believed the time had finally come to stand up for justice and righteousness in God's name on behalf of their brother and sister co-sufferers.

The Civil Rights movement did not just spring up from nothing and nowhere. It was deeply rooted in all that had

111

taken place in the history of people of African descent in the United States. The movement was the fruit of African roots and American branches and had to be woven together by many hearts, minds, and spirits into the immensely powerful tapestry of love and resistance that it became.

There has always been one constant thread in the hearts of African Americans throughout the centuries of their sojourn in the United States: the desire to experience a true physical and spiritual freedom. For them, this meant not just breaking the chains of slavery but breaking the chains of the feudal system enforced by the Jim Crow laws that were quickly forged after Reconstruction, especially in the Southern states, to re-enslave them in all but name. They sought to regain what had been promised them with the war's end and the passage of the Thirteenth, Fourteenth, and Fifteenth amendments. They sought the freedom to do as they desired with their lives, their minds, their bodies, and their spirits: to live where they chose; to vote for whomever they desired; and to educate themselves and their children in any school they desired. They sought to do so without having to live in fear of their lives being forfeit because they had unwittingly broken one of the arcane laws of Jim Crow segregation, the unique form of apartheid that continued to persevere in the United States for more than one hundred years after legal slavery's official end.

Black men and women who had found themselves caught up in the sticky web of Jim Crow voted with their feet, leaving in mass numbers for the North, Midwest, and West in what came to be known as the Great Migration.[3] Between 1915 and 1975, the equivalent of three generations, the South was emptied of millions of Blacks, the descendants of those formerly enslaved, who saw no legitimate reason for staying where they were wanted only as menial laborers and servants.

The North, Midwest, and West became the new Promised Land, just as the North had been during the period of slavery, where not only the freedom to live a decent and fairly unrestricted life could be found but also the freedom to work, to worship, to break new ground.[4] My parents were part of this great demographic shift as they left Tennessee in the early 1940s following my mother's older sister and her family. They quickly found good-paying jobs, my father in a chemical plant and my mother, like Rosie the Riveter, building aircraft wings. Those who left often still thought of the South as home, as my parents did, and regularly sent their Northern- and Western-born children "home" in the summers. Those who did not leave found myriad ways to ignore the discriminatory restrictions and soften their blows within self-determined Black communities and institutions, like churches and schools from elementary through college, so as to live a fairly self-fulfilled life but one still too often exposed to the violent whims of white folk.

It is in the South, the former states of the Confederacy, that the full extent and weight of the Jim Crow laws persisted with their stranglehold on the lives and livelihoods of thousands of men, women, and children of African descent. In many ways it is truly miraculous that African Americans survived yet another hundred years of slavery in all but name. The "Peculiar Institution" of slavery may have ended, but the even more peculiar system—peculiar because it was never formally acknowledged as such—of Jim Crow bound Blacks to land they still did not own in their own right, forcing them to work in the fields and factories of their former slave masters and their descendants.

In the former Confederate states whites sought to maintain a way of life that suited their own needs, not the needs of those they were exploiting; it was a style of life that elevated and maintained their sense of supremacy over a people fit, in their opinion, to be only beasts of burden. Cheap labor, both in the fields and in white homes, was seen as a necessity, regardless of the negative impact that it had on African American lives. Those who refused to cooperate were coerced, arrested for spurious reasons, and forced onto chain gangs that were then hired out to any who wanted "slave" labor.[5]

Often required to live where they worked, many women saw their own children infrequently, if at all. Their husbands, fathers, and sons—just like their mothers, sisters, and daughters—toiled day and night to bring in a large enough crop to sever their dependency on the white man's stores, but they rarely succeeded. Somehow, no matter how successful the planting and harvesting were, they found themselves deeper and deeper in debt because everything was controlled by whites.

With all seed, equipment, animals, food, clothing, and other necessities coming from stores owned by those for whom they worked, and with the final "toting up" done by the landowner, who decided how much the laborers had earned through their backbreaking labor, it was humanly impossible to make even a small profit. At the end of the harvest many planters would simply say that both sides had "broke even," so the laborer did not owe the planter, but neither did the planter owe the laborer. No cash exchanged hands, leaving the laborers yet again having to "borrow" food, clothing, shoes, equipment, and more seed for another season in order to survive. It was almost impossible to get ahead and be able to save for a better life. This became of critical importance beginning with World War I, when many Northern factories began soliciting the vast labor pool of the South, much to the anger of Southern planters and households.

The Black church was of critical importance to the sharecroppers as well as urban Blacks in the South and elsewhere after Reconstruction. It served as an escape from the indignities of daily life and as an anchor in what often seemed to be a stormy sea. The Black church was a refuge, a spiritual haven and oasis, a place of education and inspiration, a source of hope and a site of dignity for many. It answered their needs in countless ways. The church in which I grew up in the 1950s and 1960s, St. Luke's AME Zion in Buffalo, New York, had a gym, a banquet hall, a library, and a bowling alley. It was where I, and countless Black young people, participated in the Scouting program, gave our first musical recitals, and learned how to recite before an audience of proud parents and church members. In the haven of St. Luke's we were able to indulge our youthful mischievousness under the watchful eyes of stern but loving elders who acted as "moms and dads" to any and every Black child that crossed their paths. They taught us how to pray and taught us about Jesus, who loved us as we were. They nurtured our budding talents and provided a respite from the demands of life in a world where, even in the North, Black children were seen as "less than" and "less capable" than white children. It was also, however, a place of middle-class elitism—and this was true in both South and North—where people's acceptance was based too often on the color of their skin, their education, and the type of work they did. The churches were often divided along class and color lines, and those that had the most well-off members were the ones that preached maintenance of the status quo and avoided stirring up trouble. This was continued evidence of the dualism that persisted in Black religion between radicalism and compromise; both were critical aspects of African American survival.[6]

In the years after Reconstruction these divergent strands or tendencies in Black religion were also manifested outside of the Black churches in the larger non-church-going community and gave birth to "alternate spiritualities" that were "ambivalent about spiritual things."[7] It is this perspective that made way for the rise of many forms of Black nationalism, both religious and secular in nature, including the Nation of Islam, which will be discussed below. It also found expression in what became the secular music of African Americans and eventually all of America. The spirituals and field hollers that rose from the heartache and despair of the slaves came together in various ways to create what became the blues and jazz, two indigenous forms of American music that expressed the pain and sorrow and yet the overwhelming hope in the midst of despair that is the life of persons of African descent in the United States.[8]

A Movement of the Spirit

By the 1950s Black people in both the North and the South were becoming restless and dissatisfied with their situations in life. Many had participated in either or both World Wars and the Korean War and had experienced a freedom unlike any they had experienced before. They saw new possibilities and were impatient with old restrictions. Those in the South knew of family members who had moved to the North, Midwest, and West and who seemed to be thriving with better jobs and housing and greater freedom to express themselves and raise their children and who had the right to vote. Those in the North and West, however, were increasingly aware of the prejudice and discrimination in housing, employment, and schools that existed in these states. Although they had greater freedom than in the South, they chafed at the restrictions that still impinged upon them.

Many in the Black community were becoming critical of the role of the Black church and its passivity and compliance with racial restriction to the degree that they often did not bother to tell their pastor when they were leaving for fear he would try to make them stay put or would tell the whites.[9] They felt more could be done by the churches and people of faith to improve their lives and the world in which they lived. Traveling in Europe during the wars they were treated simply as Americans working with whites in the military and elsewhere; this opened their eyes to new possibilities and opportunities for themselves and their brothers and sisters. They began to believe real change was possible despite the harsh reaction of racist whites to Black men and women in uniform or at work beside them and, in some cases, worshiping alongside them.[10]

They had always been aware of the hypocrisy of America, but now they saw even more clearly how lies were crafted to keep them "in their place" while others reaped the benefits of the American Dream. They had fought and died for freedom since the American Revolution, but freedom was still being denied them and their children for reasons that did not stand up to the light of day.

Those who returned home to the South, hopeful for a new day, were rudely awakened from their dream of equality by lynch mobs. The upright white Christians of small and large Southern towns were determined to remind them of their "proper place" in Southern society. They used the law of shotgun and rope to enforce their message, leaving the "strange fruit" of the desecrated, disfigured, tortured bodies of Black men, women, and even children blossoming on dozens of Southern trees.[11] After Sunday church services was the favored time for these public acts of rampant terrorism where grotesque souvenirs of human body parts were cherished and postcard pictures of the event were sent around the country proclaiming the fun that was had by all, except of course the tortured Black victims.

In the aftermath of World War I, however, little could be done other than to flee the South, as many did. Without access to resources, without legal support, Blacks had few options but flight. Those who, for whatever reason, refused or were unable to leave "hunkered down," making the best of the terrible situations in which their lives and those of their children could be forfeited by an angry white person, individually or in a mob, for crimes they quite often had not committed. Slowly, things began to change in the period after the Second World War when another wave of Black soldiers and sailors, male and female, returned after seeing Europe and receiving, for the most part, unbiased treatment from its citizens. In 1941, under pressure from A. Philip Randolph's[12] threat to hold a massive march on Washington DC, President Franklin D. Roosevelt issued Executive Order 8802, which prohibited all government contractors from discriminating in their employment practices based on race, color, or national origin. President Truman's desegregation of the Armed Forces of the United States in 1948, which, by the end of the twentieth century, led to the Army being the most integrated institution in the country, was the forerunner of a renewed and determined assault on any and all laws that discriminated against persons of African descent.

This became a time of great spiritual ferment throughout the country, culminating in Montgomery, Alabama, in

1955 with the formal emergence of the Civil Rights movement. In many ways this movement was not new; it was the
manifestation once again of the more radical aspect of Black
spirituality and activism in the Black church and community. The shifts that occurred were partly in response to the
harsh reactions of whites to Black efforts and demands for
an equality that was more than token. But these shifts were
also in accordance with the "signs of the times."[13] African
Americans began seriously to challenge the status quo in
the United States just as peoples of color all over the world
were also raising similar questions of identity and situation,
demanding changes that opened doors that had for so long
been firmly closed. Colonies began to topple as the colonized
demanded independence, and Jim Crow began to wobble as
its roots were attacked through law suits instigated by the
NAACP Legal Defense Fund that demanded the desegregation
of schools, lunch counters, employment, transportation, and
any and all forms of segregated life in the United States. The
Holy Spirit, which had seemed dormant for so long a time,
was once again, many believed, spreading her wings over the
oppressed and marginalized in the world, fanning sparks of
hope and anger in the spirits and minds of countless millions
who were determined to be free, independent members of
the human race.

In the United States "the arc of the moral universe," as
Martin Luther King Jr. had affirmed, began once again to
"bend toward justice."[14] New generations of Black preachers
supported by waves of church-goers, students, and teachers
from every walk of life in the Black community began to put
their bodies on the line for freedom and raise their voices,
singing freedom songs like "Ain't gonna let nobody turn me
around, turn me around, turn me around. Ain't gonna let
nobody turn me around; I'm gonna keep on walkin', keep
on talkin', walkin' on to freedom land."

Howard Thurman and Vernon Johns were among the earliest African American ministers to challenge the state of apartheid in the United States. Thurman, especially, was a spiritual

leader who raised critical questions in the Black community concerning the role of Christianity and faith in Jesus Christ.

In the aftermath of World War II and the massive migration of Blacks, African Americans began to question their faith and its relevancy in the world of opportunity opening before them. They began to revitalize their faith in ways that reached back to their African ancestry while recontextualizing that faith in the modern era of promise and possibility. Reverend Howard Thurman began to articulate the critical questions confronting Black Christians at this time about the meaning of Christ and, therefore, of Christianity in a troubled world. Why, he asked, does it seem that Christianity is impotent to deal with "issues of discrimination and injustice on the bases of race, religion, and national origin?"[15] Thurman responded by noting that Jesus was a Jew, someone with a specific racial, ethnic, and religious identity; he was a poor Jew, placing him in solidarity with the poor of his time and of our time today; and, lastly, he was a member of an oppressed minority. All of these factors shaped Jesus and thus shaped his religion as a "direct response to the concrete sufferings of the oppressed."[16] For Thurman, Jesus is the one who sets free those oppressed and marginalized by the powers of their time. He mediates the way to the kingdom of God and he liberates those who believe in him.

Thurman's many writings, deeply contemplative in nature, sought to develop a spirituality of wholeness. His sermons and books were deeply rooted in the Black historical experience and were therefore a significant source of Black spirituality and emphasized survival and liberation. He believed God's spirit was moving in the hearts of all of humanity calling them "to act against the spirit of their times or caus[ing] them to anticipate a spirit which is yet in the making. In a movement of dedication, they are given wisdom and courage to dare a deed that challenges and to kindle a hope that inspires."[17]

Thurman's efforts to develop a fully integrated, multicultural church, the Church of the Fellowship of All Peoples (1944), where all believers in God could worship freely together, was one way of challenging racial segregation in Christian churches, Black and white. Rev. Vernon Johns used a somewhat more revolutionary approach that stirred up his parishioners (usually in opposition) and the larger white community. As the pastor of prominent middle- and upper-middle-class Black churches (including Dexter Memorial Baptist Church in Montgomery, Alabama), Johns sought to stir his congregation out of its materialistic complacency and class consciousness and to take a stand against the abusive treatment they and their brother and sister Blacks received from dominant white society. His methods were far from subtle and often caused conflict not just with his parishioners but with the dominant white society as he fiercely condemned segregation and racism as anti-Christian and called for changes in the social, political, and religious life of Southern communities.[18] He called for Christian ministers, Black and white alike, to live up to their faith, and he asked, "When will Christian preachers either preach Jesus or save the public from further deception by unfrocking themselves of his name?"[19]

Martin Luther King Jr. and the Struggle for Civil Rights

Martin Luther King Jr. was another Black church leader who saw Christianity and, therefore, Jesus Christ as radically present in the struggle for the civil rights of African Americans. King, a Baptist minister, was affected by a number of influences, including the liberal Social Gospel of Reinhold Niebuhr, the nonviolent teachings of Gandhi, and the religious and spiritual traditions of the African American church. Out of these he forged a theology of Christian nonviolent disobedience that helped to re-radicalize the Black community and the Black church and, in so doing, profoundly change the United States. King, a deeply spiritual man, believed that Jesus, the Son of God, was in solidarity with those historically oppressed and downtrodden. In the United States that meant

Black Americans, who were confronted everywhere with racism. God was a God of the poor and meek who empowered them to fight their own battle of liberation guided by Jesus the Liberator.

In Oslo, Norway, upon receiving the Nobel Peace Prize (1964), King called for a renewed understanding of nonviolence:

> Nonviolence is the answer to the crucial political and moral questions of our time—the need for mankind to overcome oppression and violence without resorting to violence and oppression. Civilization and violence are antithetical concepts. . . . Sooner or later all the people of the world will have to discover a way to live together in peace, and thereby transform this pending cosmic elegy into a creative psalm of brotherhood. If this is to be achieved, man must evolve for all human conflict a method which rejects revenge, aggression and retaliation. The foundation of such a method is love.[20]

King helped to rekindle Black America's faith in a God who walked and talked with them and a Father who sent his Son on their behalf to guide them into the new kingdom of God, the beloved community where all of humanity lived, worked, and played in harmony one with another. He lived his spirituality not only in his preaching and prayer life but also in his everyday life, and he called forth a response that in time overwhelmed the South's restrictive laws and limitations on Black life. He was the catalyst that set the river of Black frustration flowing in a nonviolent and organized manner. King saw the Black church as instrumental in the Black struggle for rights, a struggle that he later realized went beyond civil rights to encompass the rights of all of humanity. Facing opposition from his parishioners as well as from leading churchmen and churchwomen of his own and other denominations and religious faiths, he sought to bring the liberating church of the past to a new and renewed life, calling it to witness to God's demand for justice and righteousness for all regardless of skin color or economic class. He deeply believed that "injustice anywhere is a threat to justice everywhere. We are caught in an inescapable network of mutuality, tied to a single garment of destiny. Whatever affects one directly, affects all indirectly."[21]

It is in the Civil Rights movement of the 1960s, catalyzed by the Montgomery bus boycott of 1955 and 1956, that all aspects of Black spirituality, passive and radical, once more come together. The movement could be said to be the final stoking of the furnace that forged the African American Christian faithful into a living army of God. In the words of gospel singer and composer James Cleveland, once God "was through" with them, they would "come forth as pure gold."[22]

Black spirituality with its emphasis on God (God-centeredness) and sacred scripture (biblical rootedness), its Spirit-filled nature that is expressed joyfully, holistically, and contemplatively, its focus on community, and its orientation toward liberation and justice once again became the foundation upon which African Americans built all of their hopes and dreams.[23] This spirituality was expressed in powerful liturgies that emphasize prayer, song, fervent preaching, and music, above all else, soul-stirring music that lifted the participants out of their seats to dance in ecstatic joy and praise of God.

The mass meetings at various Black churches throughout the South, many of which were bombed and/or burned to the ground afterward, gathered the dispersed threads of Black spirituality and wove them once again into a tight, embracing, protective garment that clothed the nonviolent demonstrators with the armor of God as they stepped out in their marches, sit-ins, and pray-ins. Participants prayed for deliverance from the hell of Jim Crow; they prayed for the safety of those marching in defiance of the laws; and they prayed for an end to this strife. As Coretta Scott King affirmed:

Prayer was a wellspring of strength and inspiration during the civil rights movement. Throughout the movement, we prayed for greater human understanding. We prayed for the safety of our compatriots in the freedom struggle. We prayed for victory in our nonviolent protest, for brotherhood and sisterhood among people of all races, for reconciliation and the fulfillment of the Beloved Community.[24]

Both the radical and passive branches of the Black community were galvanized into action by the fires and bombings as well as the spirit-filled example of men and women like themselves, and children as young as six, very much like their own, stepping into the hands of danger by peacefully participating in the demonstrations and being viciously attacked. As the movement brought together people from all classes and across racial and gender lines for the common cause of freedom, they affirmed and authenticated their faith and their spirituality.

Jamie T. Phelps notes:

The absolute criterion of authentic black spirituality is its impact on the quality of the believer's life. It assumes that the true nature of our faith is reflected in the way in which we relate to other human beings and the created order, and that our concern for others will naturally generate witness and actions directed toward the realization of freedom for all human beings to live a liberated and joyful life, energized by the power of the Spirit.

Authentic black spirituality leads to prophetic action on behalf of justice, a justice that requires liberation from sin and its effects. . . . A person imbued with the life-force at the center of black spirituality—with the Spirit of God—is willing to struggle for this liberation.[25]

Music was of critical importance. The spirituals experienced a joyful rebirth while at the same time continuing their metamorphosis into gospel music, a more upbeat and contemporary religious sound that combined the message of scripture with the harmonies and discordances of the blues and jazz. This new music with its often socially challenging messages and urban beat helped to "stir up" the spirits of those preparing to step into unknown and dangerous territory by marching to challenge the hated Jim Crow laws. They were spread throughout the movement not only by well-known singers such as Mahalia Jackson but by folk singers, Black and white, including Odetta, Pete Seeger, and Joan Baez, who joined their voices and placed their bodies in harm's way, linking up with new groups like the Freedom Singers led by Bernice Johnson (Reagon). They also brought in older union songs, folk songs, and other songs of revolutionary fervor that with a slight shift of lyrics lifted hearts, minds, and spirits for the dangers ahead. One such song became a resounding rally-ing cry throughout the movement, the nation, and the world:

> We shall overcome.
> We shall overcome
> We shall overcome someday
> Deep in my heart
> I do believe that
> We shall overcome some day.[26]

With new lyrics composed on site, just as in the days of slavery, this song and countless others became the founda-tion for a spirituality of resistance that sustained marchers, preachers, and pray-ers alike.

The struggles of the 1950s were aided by the resounding victory in the Supreme Court of *Brown vs. Board of Educa-tion of Topeka* (1954) that denied the constitutionality of the older *Plessy vs. Ferguson* formula of "separate but equal" in the nation's schools. This decision laid a foundation for further suits protesting the constitutionality of laws that lay at the very core of Jim Crow's system of apartheid and af-fected housing, transportation, libraries, restaurants, lunch counters, and so on. The battle for the eradication of these laws proved to be a fiery crucible for Black spirituality as the hearts and minds of both Blacks and whites were caught up and transformed in ways no one would have thought possible ten years earlier.

Black Power and the Nation of Islam

Over time, however, the nonviolent movement of Martin Luther King Jr. began to lose its momentum, especially when King turned to the North in recognition of its subtle but still pervasive systems of segregation and discrimination against African Americans. Younger members of the movement grew weary of turning the other cheek while being beaten and even killed and sought more provocative and effective ways of inducing systemic change in the United States. They recognized that the issue was larger than integration, which too often became assimilation. Rather, the need was for political and economic power that would force equality, if necessary, or at least create a level playing field for all.

> The fundamental distortion facing us in the controversy about "black power" is rooted in a gross imbalance of power and conscience between Negroes and white Americans. . . . As a result, the power of white men and the conscience of black men have been corrupted. . . . Powerlessness breeds a race of beggars. We are faced now with a situation where conscienceless power meets powerless conscience, threatening the very foundations of our nation.[27]

The call for Black Power first rang out in a dusty campsite alongside the road to Montgomery in 1965 as marchers moved out from Selma after the first march was violently disrupted by local police. Although initially opposed by Dr. King, by the time of his assassination he too had come to see the connections among race, class, and other forms of oppression on a national and international plane. Although he never abandoned his philosophy of nonviolent resistance, he began to speak out on other issues besides race, including the war in Vietnam. However, he remained opposed to the violence he perceived as inherent in the Black Power movement and doubted its ability to help achieve his "dream." As he stated, "I am not interested in power for power's sake, but I'm interested in power that is moral, that is right and that is good." In words that almost echo the statement of his fellow Black churchmen, King asserts: "What is needed is a realization that power without love is reckless and abusive, and love without power is sentimental and anemic. Power at its best is love implementing the demands of justice, and justice at its best is power correcting everything that stands against love."[28]

The Black Power movement was taken up enthusiastically in the 1960s by the Nation of Islam, a pseudo-Islamic entity with great influence in the North, especially among young urban Black males. The Black Muslims combined the call for Black Power with a call for Black separation from the United States, either by a return to Africa or by the establishment of an independent Black nation in the southern part of the United States, thus helping influence the shift once again from Black Power to a resurgence of Black Nationalism.

These movements were very much in keeping with older efforts such as Marcus Garvey's Negro Improvement Association (NIA) in the early 1900s and the call, in the late 1800s, of Bishop Henry McNeal Turner and others for Blacks to return to Africa.[29] Those who were attracted to these efforts were, for the most part, fallen-away Christians or those for whom Christianity was a fraud, the "white man's religion." The majority of Blacks were unaffected because they saw the Nation of Islam as antithetical to their Christian faith. The most outspoken leader of the Nation of Islam was Malcolm X, a charismatic speaker who argued fiercely against any form of interaction or accommodation with whites.[30] His was an alternative theology/spirituality that helped kindle renewed resistance in persons of African descent, especially in the North where he was much more popular with the young than was King.

Whether simply seeking access to the corridors of power within the United States or a complete overhaul of the system and separation from it, Black Nationalists and Black Power advocates often found their message taken to the extremes of violence by their followers. In the aftermath of the assassination of King, Blacks across the United States destroyed acres of homes and businesses in city after city in an outpouring of frustrated rage.

Although these movements were successful in bringing greater attention to bear upon the economic, social, and political disparities between Blacks and whites, they also raised questions among many as to how far was too far to go in demanding such change. Was violence the only answer? A resounding no came from another group of young Black men, attracted like many to the demands for Black Power but categorically opposed to the idea of Black Nationalism and separation. They were young men in the Protestant denominations, for the most part fresh out of seminary, who sought to make their voices heard in the debate raging among the different perspectives now found in the Black community and to articulate a new way of thinking about God and Jesus Christ. Included were James H. Cone and Gayraud S. Wilmore.

The clash between the theology of the Civil Rights movement and the secular political/sociological critique of the Black Power movement led to a more fully articulated Black Christology that emerged as part of a slowly developing Black theology of liberation. These new perspectives deeply influenced the spirituality of the Black church and its members. It is here we see the first blooming of the radically Black church that Wilmore described, one for whom faith in Jesus Christ meant faith in a God who acted in human history to free those oppressed simply because of who they were, the least among us. Prior to this development, most Blacks, including ministers, did not have the education or the interest in formulating a theology of, by, and for African Americans. There were too many other urgent issues to be addressed instead of what then seemed a luxury.[31] They had preached, prayed, and sung their theology then, but now, in the latter part of the 1960s, using newly acquired tools garnered in theological seminaries, it was necessary to build a theological structure they could use to defend the faith that was theirs (1 Pt 3:15). In so doing, a new theological understanding emerged, one still rooted in the Black historical experience but able to articulate the meaning of God and Jesus Christ in Black lives in the United States in theological language understandable to Blacks and whites alike.

> Black Theology is a theology of black liberation. It seeks to plumb the black condition in the light of God's revelation in Jesus Christ, so that the black community can see that the gospel is commensurate with the achievement of black humanity. Black theology is a theology of "blackness." It is the affirmation of black humanity that emancipated black people from white racism, thus providing authentic freedom for both white and black people. It affirms the humanity of white people in that it says No to the encroachment of white oppression.[32]

A Liberating Black Theology

Black theology emerged from a generation of Black ministers younger than King and his supporters. They saw the limitations of King's nonviolent movement in a country where violence seemed almost natural, but they were opposed to what they saw as the unchristian violence of the Black Power and Black Nationalism protagonists. They saw the need to focus on political and economic issues rather than just social ones, while recognizing that the issue of race, the color of one's skin, colored all such discussions.[33]

Several persons were critical in this evolution, including Black ministers James H. Cone, Gayraud S. Wilmore, Albert Cleage, and J. Deotis Roberts, among others. As they sought to reconcile the call for the political and economic empowerment of the Black community that was at the heart of the call for Black Power with the teachings of Christianity, they found it necessary to raise questions regarding Jesus' being and salvific purpose that had been raised by generations before them but accepted on faith. Now they saw the need to articulate more clearly that faith for the benefit of, most important, their brother and sister Black Christians but also for all Americans, regardless of race or ethnicity: Who is Jesus for African Americans today? Is God truly on the side of the oppressed, or is he simply a white racist, siding with those who have historically oppressed Blacks? What is the significance of Jesus' life, death, and resurrection for African Americans? Can African Americans remain Christians in light of their ongoing situation of racist oppression, or is Christianity simply a religion of whites? For most, the responses to these questions affirmed the liberative role of Jesus in their lives. However, there were different contextual perspectives, which emerged as two christological strands. The first, sociopolitical in nature, focused on Jesus as the messiah, the Son of humankind and thus the liberator of oppressed humanity, while the second, the spiritual/cultural strand, emphasized the understanding of Jesus as the Christ (the Son of God), the mediator between the forces of sin and evil and the forces of good.

Cone, a Methodist minister, from small town Bearden, Arkansas, articulates the sociopolitical meaning of Jesus Christ as liberator. Questioning the absence of the historical and religious experience of Blacks in his theological studies, he sought to understand and articulate Jesus' significance for Blacks by arguing that Jesus is the Black Christ. Christ's blackness refers to both his own victimization and his victory. Blackness is the bridge between the historical first-century Jesus and the Christ proclaimed by the faithful. The blackness of Jesus for Cone is a comprehensive theological truth. Jesus and, therefore, God are Black because only as Black are they in full solidarity with those who, especially in the United States, have historically been oppressed simply because they are Black.[34] As a Black man, Christ "really enters into our world where the poor, the despised, and the black are, disclosing that he is with them, enduring their humiliation and pain and transforming oppressed slaves into liberated servants."[35]

Jesus is ontologically Black because blackness is a manifestation of God's being revealing for Blacks that neither divinity nor humanity reside in white definitions but in liberation from captivity. In later writings, as he interacted with liberation theologians from other cultural contexts and womanist theologians in the Black community, Cone's understanding of Jesus' role as liberator expanded to encompass all who were oppressed because of their race, gender, class, or sexual orientation.

Gayraud S. Wilmore's understanding of Jesus is deeply grounded in the African American historical and cultural experience. Sacred scripture, he argues, has to be contextualized and reclaimed by persons of color in order to transcend and transform the color bias historically inherent in Christianity. For Wilmore, the blackness of Jesus as the Black Messiah invests blackness with religious meaning that reveals the reality of Black suffering in the historical experience of Black people in a racist society. "The black Messiah is both a concrete incarnation of God among people of color who cannot be understood apart from their experience, and a comprehensive symbol of the divine presence whose revelatory power is available to all."[36] The Black Messiah critiques the racism of biblical religion and of the political order.

J. Deotis Roberts emphasizes Jesus as the mediator whose blackness is symbolic rather than ontological. His discussion of the relationship between the Black Messiah and the Christ of faith reveals the former as a mythical construct necessary to counteract the negativity associated with blackness. The

Black Messiah is, particularly in light of the universal Christ of scripture, serving as a frame of reference through which Blacks can comprehend the teachings of Christianity. The Black Messiah delivers a kind of psycho-cultural and experiential liberation whose ultimate goal is the reconciliation of all believers in the reign of Christ, which is spiritual rather than political.

Finally, Albert Cleage espoused the most radical Christology, arguing that Jesus is not simply ontologically or symbolically Black but that he is truly physically Black, a Black Jew who lived in a Black nation (Israel) and fought the status quo of Roman imperialism. Jesus "came to free a Black people from the oppression of the white Gentiles."[37] Cleage founded the Shrine of the Black Madonna, which articulated the belief that Jesus was born of a Black woman, was Black physically, and was directly engaged in liberative action on the side of the oppressed Blacks in the form of Black Nationalism.

Cone, Wilmore, Roberts, and Cleage would all agree that just as Black theology is a liberating theology, so Black spirituality is a liberating spirituality. As Carlyle Stewart Fielding has observed, "African American spirituality has been instrumental in giving black people the spiritual and cultural elements to liberate themselves from those internal tyrannies that sequester the soul and destroy the mind."[38]

All of these discussions influenced the varying threads of spirituality found within the African American community as well as the identity of Black Americans as witnessed by changes in the way they were named: from *colored* and *Negro* to *Afro-American* and *Black* and finally to *African American*. These shifts and turns forced Blacks, lay and clergy alike, religious and secular of every faith and religion, to grapple with questions of identity: Who am I? Who are we as a people? Why have we had to struggle for so long a time for basic freedoms that should be accorded to all human beings? Where do we go from here? As they began to articulate their understanding of God and Jesus in their own images and recognize themselves in the Holy, they were, for the most part, reaffirmed in their faith. The dream of their ancestors was finally in sight for their descendants. Their belief in a "wonderworking God" was finally reaching fulfillment.

The Praxis of Black Catholics

During this time, Black Catholics were not simply passive observers of what was taking place but actively participated in the Civil Rights movement while initiating demands for rights and freedoms long withheld in the Roman Catholic Church. The period of the 1960s and 1970s in the Roman Catholic Church was one of rapid transformation and challenge. The Civil Rights movement, albeit begun mainly in the Protestant Christian churches, quickly found willing Catholics adding their voices and their bodies to the cause. Black religious men and women, such as Sister Antona Ebo, who marched at Selma, joined priests and laity of every race and ethnicity who were actively involved in the marches, sit-ins, demonstrations, and demands for justice and equality for African Americans, which challenged white dominant society, both politically and religiously, in the United States. However, many had to participate against the will of their bishop or superior, and it must be admitted that the U.S. church itself "made no substantial contribution to this organized effort."[39]

At the same time the Civil Rights movement began to be overshadowed by the more radical Black Power and Black Nationalist movements, Catholics found their own church emerging from Vatican II (1963–65), a historic council that called it to a greater openness to the faithful and a recognition of the significance of the different and equally valid cultures from which the faithful came. The church was returned to the people of God by the turning of altars to face the congregation and the celebration of the Eucharist in English and other vernacular languages. Black Catholics, inspired by these changes and those wrought by the Civil Rights movement, began to reassert their own claim to recognition and affirmation of their four hundred-plus years of faithfulness in and for the church, as well as their right to celebrate their faith and worship in a style and manner in keeping with their culture and history.

The National Black Catholic Congresses of the nineteenth century,[40] organized and run by lay Catholics, gave way to the formation of groups that spoke with the voices of more than three million Black Catholics who spoke to church and world of the racism and sexism found within their mother church. In 1968, the first gathering of Black priests took place. They issued a statement declaring that the "Roman Catholic Church is a white racist institution."[41] While participating in demonstrations side by side with their Protestant brothers and sisters, they demanded changes in their mother church. They formed independent bodies to speak and agitate on their belief and interacted with Black Protestant theologians in the development of Black theology. Black Catholics looked back to Africa and their presence in the early church as well as their own experiences of diaspora and slavery to begin to forge a Black Catholic theology of liberation.

The spirituality of Black Catholics is a sacramental spirituality grounded in their own historical experience and that of all African Americans but also interwoven with the rituals and teachings of their faith. At its core is the Eucharist, the coming together as a people, a community, to share the Bread of Life. At the communion table there should be no races, genders, or ethnicities, no hierarchy, no inequality. Yet for centuries that had been their experience—forced to sit in the balconies and to wait until all others had participated before they could receive the Body and Blood of Christ. This was a denial of their human dignity as persons created in the image and likeness of God. They found themselves in a double bind as Blacks and as Catholics. Theologian Jamie T. Phelps has summarized this experience:

African American Catholics experience a double invisibility, marginalization and devaluation. In the Black world we are marginalized because of our religious identity as Catholics, and in the Catholic world we are marginalized because of our racial identity as African Americans. . . . Black Catholics simply wish to make it possible to be Black, Catholic, and American without being cursed and spit upon, devalued and marginalized by other Blacks, Catholics, or Americans.[42]

Yet Black Catholics, like Black Protestants, persevered in their faith and reclaimed their spiritual and cultural heritage as they began to formulate a Black Catholic theology of liberation that spoke of and to their struggles and to devise liturgies that partook of the richness of their blackness.

Despite their emphasis on the Black community and its needs and concerns, a glaring absence existed in the early work of these male theologians. None raised or discussed in any way the role of Black women, despite the seminal presence of Black women in every freedom movement developed by the Black community. The contributions of women were either taken for granted or overlooked. The absence of women's voices became even more obvious as the women's movement began to expand in the 1970s and 1980s and women of all races and ethnicities began to enter seminaries and theologates. Just as the civil rights, Black Power, and Black Nationalism movements catalyzed and mirrored the myriad liberation movements of colonized and subjected persons throughout the globe, women also began to raise questions of their own in the church, a theme discussed in Chapter 7.

How Far We've Come

In the latter part of the twentieth century African Americans began to reflect fully on their journey and sought to answer the question of "how we got over." How, they wondered as they looked back over the centuries, had they as a people been able to survive, to have children, to pass on their culture and traditions, and build viable communities of faith and hope? Their faith in a God of justice and righteousness, in brother Jesus the liberator, and sister Spirit who nurtured and sustained them on their long and painful journeying, enabled them to develop a spirituality, a relationship with their God that emphasized survival, resistance, and liberation against any and all odds.

In *And Still We Rise* I described the outcome of generations of struggle:

> God and Jesus are not problematical [for Black Christians]; they are both immanent and transcendent in our lives. The immanent God loves us and nurtures us like a parent bending low over a child, yet as transcendent God is free to judge those who oppress us and call us forth into freedom. Jesus as immanent humanity is brother, sister and friend; he is in all ways one with us, walking and talking with us, sharing our journey, and carrying our burdens, and suffering the pain of our oppression and rejection, yet as transcendent Son of God, he will come forth in glory to lead us to the Promised Land. And we rejoice in the Holy Spirit, that balm of Gilead sent to heal our sin-sick souls, to abide within us and to strengthen us on our journey while giving us the courage to fight back against our oppressors and to "keep on keepin' on."[43]

Regardless of the nature and makeup of individual Black communities, whether Protestant or Catholic, Muslim or secular, faith abided. This was a deep-seated faith. Even though many in more secular settings scoffed at the "doings" of church folk, this faith still spoke, cried, and sang with spiritual undertones of a better world to come, a world where there would be no more pain or sorrow.

By the end of the twentieth century Black communities were still under challenge from economic, political, and persistent racial woes, but they were also, for the most part, still intact and progressing. Once again, in the face of battles won and lost, their spirituality underwent transformation as different voices sought different ends, yet all were still grounded in the Black historical and religious experience, including those who rejected some aspects of that experience.

New strands began to emerge as Blacks moved away from Christianity to experience religions such as Buddhism and Hinduism as well as Islam. Others sought a return to their African roots and made connections with the growing number of Africans migrating, voluntarily this time, from many African nations and bringing their indigenous religions with them, especially the Yoruba tradition. Others strayed from religion of any kind or belief in any form of transcendent Other, seeking a personal spirituality without ties to any form of institutionalized religion. Still others denied faith of any kind, and there were also some who became involved with the Afro-Catholic religions of Haiti (Vodoun), Cuba and Puerto Rico (Santería), and Brazil (Candomblé).

And some who had prospered as a result of the civil rights and other movements—and had been able to attain the education, jobs, and homes they had sought for so long—embraced a new theology, one that harked back in many ways to the Puritanism of the early seventeenth and eighteenth centuries with its emphasis on acquiring wealth and seeing and seeking God's blessings in material ways.

Despite these shifts and the growing schisms within the community arising from growing class and cultural differences,

> the radical faiths of Malcolm and King coalesce in the opaque depths of a Black spirituality that is neither Protestant nor Catholic, Christian nor Islamic in its essence, but comprehends and transcends all these ways of believing and worshiping by experiencing God's real presence in the search for justice, by becoming one with God in suffering, struggle, and in the celebration of the liberation of the whole creation.[44]

7

Beautiful Are the Souls
of My Black Sisters

The Spirituality
of African American Women[1]

The night is beautiful,
So the faces of my people, . . .

Beautiful, also, is the sun,
Beautiful, also, are the souls of my people.
— LANGSTON HUGHES[2]

Daughters of Africa

Enslaved Black women were especially important in the retention and passing down of Black culture. Both womanist and Black feminist scholars[3] use the phrase *bearers of culture* to depict the role they played in their communities. They taught much needed skills and also preserved African traditions of song and story, thereby helping to develop, nurture, and perpetuate the emerging Black community during slavery and after. They also knew how to bide their time and "hunker down" until a better time for action arose rather than risk lives in a futile gesture of rebellion. For Black women, liberation was not the only goal, nor was it the most important goal. These women recognized their need to survive as the most important factor and then their need to have a reasonable quality of life while still enslaved so that they and their families could indeed survive until freedom was theirs.[4]

Responsible as they were for the lives of all in the slave community, but especially for the children, slave women resorted to numerous ways of teaching the skills of literacy, survival, the healing arts, and the necessary crafts to those around them. In doing so, they helped not only to preserve their community but also to strengthen it. They lived an active spirituality of resistance in their lives, using various means to maintain their bodily and spiritual integrity.[5]

All Black women living in the United States today are daughters of Africa who, over a period of almost five hundred years, were perfected as women of God.[6] We do not know the names of most of our ancestral mothers who were brought to these shores against their will, but their stories, songs, and prayers live on in their descendants today. Brought to a new and very strange land, they found themselves separated from family and friends, from those who understood their language and shared their culture, and sold to serve as breeders, field hands, wet nurses, and maids of all kinds. Cuffed and shackled, they were taken to distant farms and plantations and quickly realized that this was to be their fate in life: to work from "can't see" before dawn until "can't see" after dusk alongside their men; to be treated as farm animals, mere beasts of labor; to be bred only to see their offspring sold away from them over and over again; to live and die as property. Women of African descent were denied the protected pedestal of the "cult of true womanhood." This understanding was used to protect but also to confine white women; to stress piety, purity, submissiveness, and domesticity for women; and to emphasize innocence and modesty. African American women, free and slave, were precluded from this understanding because they were required to work in the same fields or at many of the same backbreaking tasks as their men.

Yet they did not despair. Nor did they turn away from all hope. They had not come empty handed to this new world because they had brought with them a deep and abiding faith in a God of creation, a God of justice and honor, even though God would have been named differently in their particular communities. They brought with them a shared worldview that, when synchretized with aspects of the Christian faith of their captors, enabled them to survive. They lived sustained by their belief in a "wonderworking" God who would, in God's own time, free them from the unmerited captivity in which they passed their weary existence.

Black women saw the world as sacred and thus resisted the dualistic separation of the sacred and secular domains that their captors and enslavers sought to instill in them. Men and women "knew" God intimately as active. This knowledge of God or God's intermediaries nurtured and sustained them in their everyday struggles. Religion was all pervasive, surrounding and bearing them up on all sides. The holy was a constant presence in their lives, and all of life was sacred, from womb to tomb, before and beyond, weaving a web of connections that encompassed both the living and the dead.

Their religious understanding helped them to create community among themselves as tribal allegiances and enmities were not viable in the Americas. Yet some kind of communal solidarity was needed as individualism was not a part of their self-understanding. It was the "we" of family and friends—real and fictive kin who played substantial roles in their lives and in the lives of their descendants—that subsumed the "I." They took these understandings and wove them into their reception of the God of Jesus Christ who, they believed, had suffered like them and shared in their pain. This God had freed others wrongly enslaved, including the Hebrews, and despite the insistence of their owners that God had willed their captive status, they knew that God would in time free them as well. They fully identified with the Hebrew people and saw themselves as God's new chosen people.

Black women, especially those who were mothers and grandmothers, were and remain a critical part of the Black community's religious and spiritual history. They were able to form a connection that, rather than being broken, was strengthened and expanded in the Americas to encompass all who were enslaved.

As Bernice Johnson Reagon affirms:

> [Mothers—biological or otherwise—] were the heads of their communities, the keepers of the tradition. The lives of these women were defined by their culture, the needs of the community and the people they served. Their lives are available to us today because they accepted responsibility when the opportunity was offered—when they were chosen. There is the element of transformation in all of their work. Building communities within societies that enslaved Africans, they and their people had to exist in, at least, dual realities. These women, however, became central to evolving the structures for resolving areas of conflict and maintaining, sometimes creating, an identity that was independent of a society organized to exploit natural resources, people, and land.[7]

These structures remain to this day as symbols of the strength, courage, and steadfast faith of these nameless and unknown African women who laid the foundation for the millions who followed. Despite the restrictions placed upon their lives and their very bodies,[8] they persisted in finding and at times forging a "way out of no way" for themselves and those they loved. Their Bible learning was orally based with verses, stories, and sayings memorized and passed down from mother to daughter and to as many others as they could gather around them. They built a foundation for the Black community grounded upon faith in a God of compassion and in God's son, Jesus, who, like them, suffered unjustly and was lynched for crimes he had not committed.

In her seminal work on African American Christian women, *Jesus, Jobs, and Justice*, Bettye Collier-Thomas sees that in their acceptance of

> the Christian virtues as the basis for the formulation of character, African American women forged an ethic for the formation of black womanhood that defined the manner in which they would survive in an alien and strange land—America. . . . By uplifting Christian virtues and clinging to a boundless faith, they measured their value and worth in God's human family.[9]

These virtues were justice, love, faith, wisdom, and perseverance, and as literacy increased among them, they looked to the scriptures for role models they could emulate. They found women like Hagar, Zipporah, Rahab, the queen of Sheba, the Canaanite woman, and others—all women they believed to be of African descent. Their concern was to see how these women who were oppressed, marginalized, and often brutalized like themselves were yet able to play significant roles in God's unfolding story of salvation.[10]

The question of the psalmist, "The Lord is my light and my salvation, whom shall I fear?" is, in actuality, more a statement of the undying and unselfconscious faith that can be said to serve as the foundation of African American women's spirituality. It is a spirituality that arises from a deep and abiding faith in a God of love, a wonderworking God who walked and talked with them, giving them the strength to persevere. This God in whom they placed not only their trust but also their very lives as slaves and second-class citizens in the United States for over four hundred years was a God transformed and transforming. Creator of all that existed, God was also a man-child in need of their love, trust, and nurturing, a spirit of strength and perseverance that guided them over the rock-strewn paths on which they were forced to travel, and a liberating, righteous lover of justice who opposed the oppression and the blasphemy of those who claimed that God was on the oppressor's side. They knew better, for they knew God personally, intimately.

Historically, persons of African descent in the United States have been, in the words of Zora Neale Hurston, a people whose eyes were always watching God. This faith in a God of love and justice gave them the strength to "keep on keepin' on," knowing that "His eye is on the sparrow and I know He watches me."[11] Nothing was too hard for God, and as a result, nothing was too hard for them to attempt to accomplish in their everyday struggle to keep hope and love alive.

Building Community

African American women's spirituality is deeply rooted in a community of the born, the yet to be born, and those who have already passed over. This community forms a great cloud of witnesses who help to shape and form all of the people into the human beings God intended them to be. Life outside of the community was inconceivable; life over against the community was suicidal. The community, from smallest child to oldest elder, was the life blood of each and every individual within it, regardless of age, gender, or ranking, and each person owed a responsibility to others within that community to enable both the community and individuals to survive and to thrive.

Faith in God and in their community of shared faith and oppression gave enslaved women hope, enabling them to persevere against daunting obstacles that threatened not simply their identity but their very lives. Somehow they were able to forge a spirituality, a holistic pervasive understanding of the interconnectedness and interdependence of all of creation with God, that has now persisted for centuries.

African American women's wisdom emerges from an experience of triple (or more) oppression. Denied the dignity of womanhood, condemned for their skin color, whether too dark or too light, and often imprisoned by mis-education, demeaning and meaningless work, and a denial of their very humanity, African American women have yet managed to forge a spirituality of hope and survival that has sustained them for centuries.

As Alice Walker noted, they dreamed dreams and had visions; they imagined a time and place when the pain and indignity of their lives would be transcended, not in some far-off heaven but right here in the future of their children and their children's children.[12] Somehow our foremothers persisted in their faith. They made rosaries out of beads and knotted string and learned scripture by rote memory. They resisted as best they could anything and anyone who attempted to keep them from living their faith on a daily basis.

Once freedom, so-called, came, they struggled, despite the callous disregard of their fellow Christians, to remain faithful. When their children were forbidden entry into diocesan or public schools, when they were required to sit in upper galleries and back pews, when they had to wait until last to partake of the sacraments, they did not suffer these indignities quietly but often walked out and with their meager resources built their own schools and church buildings.[13]

African American women wove a tapestry of love, faith, and hope that they wrapped around any and all who came into their lives, much as Harriet Tubman, the general of the Underground Railroad, did. Harriet "created" family wherever she was, as many other slaves did. They re-created communities to replace those from which they were torn through the Middle Passage; the sale of their husbands, parents, and/or children; and the willful destruction of their culture and traditions by those threatened by and fearful of it.[14]

Tubman, after spending much of her adult life bringing her fellow slaves out of bondage, continued after slavery's end to care for those linked to her by their experiences of slavery. "She took in elderly and sick slaves, former slaves, and basically anyone who came to her door who had nowhere to go and no resources or help whatsoever. She created her own welfare system for the stranger and the poor by inviting them to live in her home and going out to work in order to feed them."[15]

As the bearers of many burdens, chosen and unchosen, African American women were also the givers of life and the teachers of the future. They suckled their children with a passionate anger and courage that sustained the hope that always dwelled within them "despite" and "through" it all.

Drawing upon a womanist perspective on Hagar, the concubine of the patriarch Abraham, Delores Williams likens Hagar's experience of surrogacy and suffering to that of the slave women, women who, despite all they were forced to endure, like Hagar, found favor with God, who helped them to survive: "The social process in the antebellum slave community turned black motherhood into something totally different from what was thought to be the model of motherhood in white society."[16]

As Williams explains:

> It was the black mother who often protected the children and family as far as they could be protected during slavery. It was a black female nurturer, called Moses by her people, who led regiments and scouted for the Union Army. . . . Sometimes it was the slave mother who was given permission by the slave master to operate her own business and thereby provide economic security for her children. . . .
>
> Incorporated, then, within the mothering and nurturing functions of slave women were the tasks of protecting, providing for, resisting oppression and liberating.[17]

African American Women and the Bible

For slave women God was a resource that sustained them in ways that the Black man or slave community often could not. Many slave women, as depicted especially in the slave narratives, exhibited a "vigorous spiritual self-confidence even though their sexuality has been completely brutalized and exploited by men of every social class."[18] As both female and slave, Black women endured all that was a part of life because "they believed there was 'nobody in the wide world to look to but God.'"[19]

They took their stand on the Bible, both Hebrew and New Testaments, seeing within its pages women like themselves who faced adversity yet rallied themselves and their communities. Using a womanist critical lens—that is, through the eyes and experience of Black women—a story heard countless times can be read and understood quite differently. What are the models of womanhood and femininity that historically have been such a significant part of Christianity's teachings on women? Mary, the mother of God, is contrasted eternally with either Eve, the alleged cause of humanity's fall into sin, or Mary Magdalene, the repentant sinner, while Hagar, a slave, is rarely mentioned at all. But these women were not so different from one another as they have been portrayed. Reading Genesis and Luke with a critical womanist eye allows us to see something very different from what has been historically taught.

Hebrew Scriptures

We have been taught that Adam and Eve were expelled from the Garden of Eden because of their disobedience in seeking to acquire knowledge. But as we read from a womanist perspective, Eve's story becomes not one of sinfulness or willful disobedience but one of a woman and man coming into the fullness of their humanity as equals, sharing the responsibilities God laid upon them, and preparing the way for those of us who come after them. For without them, would we even be? Beginning appropriately with the text of Genesis and the second Creation story (Gn 2:4–25), we find that nowhere in that story does it say that Eve committed a sin (actually her son, Cain, was the first sinner because he first committed murder), nor is she cursed by God (only the serpent is), nor can it be said that she seduced or in any other way forced Adam to eat of the fruit of the tree in the garden's center. Ironically, she is the first person in the Bible to serve someone food (something women have been doing from then on). But she and Adam are expelled from the garden because they have acquired knowledge; that is, they have become thinking, aware human beings. It could be said that they have become fully human.

Yet many if not most interpretations of this story place fault solely with Eve, who, in actuality, is a woman guilty, if of anything, only of seeking greater knowledge than was deemed good for her. From a womanist perspective, as the descendant of a people forbidden to learn how to read and write at pain of death but also, ironically, stigmatized as incapable of learning, Eve's story is one not of sin but of courage and boldness. It is a story of persistence in the pursuit of knowledge, a persistence rewarded by an increase of pain (whether in childbirth or in struggling to learn under almost impossible conditions after a day of backbreaking labor), a pain deemed worthy of repeating (as women do by bearing more than one child and our enslaved ancestors did by persisting in their efforts to gain an education despite whippings, beatings, and being burned out of their homes and schools). The pain is overcome by the reward of greater knowledge, a goal historically deemed worthy of pursuit only by men.

The other woman whose example provides Black women with hope for the journey is Hagar, the Egyptian slave. Her story is told in Genesis 16:1–16 and 21:9–21. Hagar, the slave woman of Sarai and then concubine of Abraham, exemplifies Black women's experience of survival in Africa and throughout the diaspora. She experiences what womanist theologian Delores Williams names the "wilderness experience," an experience that all African Americans have shared in slavery and afterward. Sadly, some Black women may still be experiencing it today. Hagar's experience revealed the wilderness not as something to be overcome or conquered but as a place of refuge. In her first wilderness experience, "[Hagar] meets *her* God for the first time. Her experience with this God could be regarded as positive by African Americans because God promises survival, freedom and nationhood for Hagar's progeny. The African-American community has, all of its life, struggled for survival, freedom, and nationhood."[20]

But Hagar's experience, like that of most slave women, does not end here. Having run away and been told by God to return to slavery so as to give birth to her son, Ishmael, she is forced once again to return to the wilderness as a free woman with her child but without resources of any kind, just as the slaves experienced a "freedom" in name only at Reconstruction's end. Williams notes: "Like African-American people, Hagar and her child are alone without resources for survival. Hagar must try to make a living in the wide, wide world for herself and her child. This was also the task of many African-American women and the entire community of black freedpeople when emancipation came."

She continues:

> The post-bellum notion of wilderness (with Hagar and child as its content) emphasized black women's and the black community's negative economic experience of poverty and social displacement. . . . This post-bellum African-American symbolic sense of wilderness, with Hagar at its center, makes the female figure symbolic of the entire black community's history of brutalization during slavery; of fierce survival struggle and economic servitude after liberation; of children being cheated out of their inheritance by oppressors; of threat to the life and well-being of the family; of the continuing search for a positive, productive quality of life for women and men under God's care.[21]

Hagar is unique in the Bible for she, a slave woman, sees and names God. She called out to God to save her child, and God responded. She named God El-roi, the God who sees (me), and like Abraham, she was told that she would be the mother of a nation (Gn 21:13, 18), the Arabic people. In today's world the wilderness experience of Hagar persists in the lives of many Black women. God reveals in Hagar's story God's love of justice and God's preferential option for the poor and the marginalized.

The New Testament

Women in the New Testament were also critical to the spirituality and faith of Black women. Like Eve, Mary Magdalene has been maligned down through the ages. For centuries venerated as the Great Apostle and the Apostle to the Apostles because of her unique presence at the resurrection as well as being commissioned by the resurrected Christ himself to spread the good news, the gospel, to others, she was unceremoniously demoted and commingled with other unnamed women in the New Testament, transformed into a prostitute and a repentant sinner. This is a stigma that remains to the present day despite the Catholic Church's quiet reversal of that commingling in 1969 when, in the process of revising the liturgical calendar, the Gospel reading for the Magdalene's feast day (July 22) was changed from that of the sinful woman (Lk 7:36–50) to that of John 20, where Mary Magdalene discovers the empty tomb. During his papacy, John Paul II acknowledged her, once again, as the Great Apostle.

From a womanist perspective the Magdalene speaks for and to countless unnamed Black women, slave and free, who were and continue to be condemned for their allegedly "sluttish" behavior. Black women today must still live down the slander of being "Jezebels," women with allegedly uncontrollable sexual appetites, as well as "Sapphires" or "sistas with attitude," in the newest permutation of the same aspersion. They are women who are willing to stand on their faith in themselves and their God in order to speak words of truth to their people and anyone else that needs to hear. Their words may seem harsh and at times unloving, but they are spoken out of love and the effort to give life. Historically, they are the ones who have done the hard and often dirty work of building family and community and passing down their people's culture—the stories, songs, prayers, and faith that helped mold them into a spiritual, faith-filled people.

First and foremost in the New Testament, however, is the story of the Virgin Mary. For two millennia we have been taught as women to revere and model ourselves after Mary meek and mild, who humbly bowed her head and submitted unquestioningly to the will of God. But looking at this story from a womanist perspective enables a different interpretation. In today's understanding Mary is still a child, barely into her teens. She is betrothed to a much older man, as was the custom of the day. She is approached by the angel Gabriel, who speaks words both mysterious and frightening. But she does not simply accept what the angel has said to her, as Luke 1:26–38 makes clear. Mary questions Gabriel, for she is understandably "troubled" by his words. She is then told that, having found favor with God, she will conceive and bear a son whom she will call Jesus. Like many women, slave and free, Mary is basically being told what her life will be. Yet again, and probably to the angel's amazement, she questions. She wants to know how this is possible, how it will come about. Gabriel's response is intended to resolve her fears and confusion once and for all but, at the same time, remind her of the power of God. Finally, he tells her that her cousin Elizabeth, who Mary knows is not only barren but also beyond her childbearing years, has also conceived and is in her sixth month of pregnancy. Only then does Mary agree to the miracle about to unfold within her.

What is the significance of all of this? First, like Hagar, Mary was spoken to directly rather than through her husband, father, uncle, or other male. At the same time, she did not seek permission from a man for her response, her "let it be done." Mary, though betrothed, was still a young virgin who knew the harsh customs of her people and the consequences of being found pregnant prior to having been wed.

She would be taken outside of her village and stoned to death. She knew, therefore, that what she was being asked to accept could cost her her life and derail her engagement to Joseph.

We read the annunciation story in just a few minutes, but for Mary it surely took much more time to make such a momentous decision. God does not force anyone; we, as humans, freely acquiesce to God's will, but we do so, not blindly, but knowing that saying yes to God will irrevocably change our lives; there will certainly be consequences. And, indeed, the life of this young woman is changed forever, as is all of history. It can also be argued that, still unsure and even perhaps a bit disbelieving of all that has taken place, she quickly goes to visit Elizabeth to see for herself evidence of God's word (Lk 1:39–56).

It is only when Mary encounters a heavily pregnant Elizabeth that she proclaims her faith in God in a magnificent song that stands to this day as a proclamation not of passivity or humility but of revolutionary hope and faith, of a reversal of the status quo and the breaking forth of God's righteous justice into the world. Mary's song, like other songs by women in sacred scripture, is not a song of pious submission but of righteous judgment and vindication for all who are born poor and oppressed and unjustly victimized. Mary prophesies about the coming reign of God, a time and place where those who are poor will receive God's bounty and those who are hungry will be fed while the rich and arrogant, those who are unjust and self-righteous, will be cast away. Is it any wonder that her son, Jesus, makes an almost identical prophetic statement in his first sermon (Lk 4:16–30)?

By saying yes to God, Mary breaks open human history and subverts it, turning all of reality upside down. She affirms and acknowledges that the miraculous work of God brought about through the Holy Spirit will result in a new reality for all of humanity. She stands, therefore, as a symbol of hope and courage for so many women, poor and invisible, who, by their actions throughout history, by their willingness to stand up and walk out on faith, like so many Black women have done, bring about a new and better world for all of humanity. They and their children serve as catalysts for change in the world and for hope beyond it. Therefore, Mary can be seen as a sign of contradiction and a model not of passivity or voicelessness, but a model for bold, daring, audacious, and courageous Black women.

As the retelling of these scriptural stories has hopefully revealed, for persons of color, especially those of African descent in the United States, the Bible has been a source of inspiration as well as an instrument of oppression—depending on who does the interpreting. Bettye Collier-Thomas expands on this, noting that

> many women viewed the Bible as a source of inspiration. It became an instrument of freedom and survival and a tool for development of literacy. Within the confines of slavery black women developed boundless spirituality and adopted the Bible as their guide, and Jesus Christ as their personal savior. Slave owners and southern white church leaders attempted to limit and shape the Christian experiences of the enslaved. Ignoring the white master's central text, "Slaves, obey your Masters," over a period of many generations black women and men molded and shaped Christianity into a complex mixture with a critical theological perspective that reinforced their sense of identity, self-worth, and personal dignity, while emphasizing freedom.[22]

For today's Black women, the Bible remains a source of inspiration and also a challenge as we continue to struggle with its teachings, seeking to understand them in today's very different contexts. Women today are named by and name themselves, not bound by the wishes or actions of father, husband, uncle, or son. Yet, as Black women, seeking to build and rebuild the Black community, we are also very much aware that, as did so many women in scripture, we must work with our men in order for all of us to not only survive but thrive. Ours is not a struggle against men but against any and all forms of oppression that hinder and/or limit us and those whom we love.

Reading the Bible with a woman's eyes, and especially the eyes of a Black woman, opens our horizons to a new awareness and new possibilities. It breaks apart the old patriarchal vision of women, allowing us to see our sisters in their sorrows and their joys, their triumphs and their failures, their self-doubt and their self-assertion. Today, as during slavery, Black women read of the myriad women of the Bible, both named and unnamed, and see themselves in their lives. These women mirror strength, courage, perseverance, industry, faith, charity, and hope for us today. They were not passive, subservient, and silent for the most part but active, vocal, and assertive. They help us to see the possibilities and opportunities that lie before us while helping us also to withstand the trials and tribulations that we continue to experience.

They are truly our sisters, these named and unnamed women who gave birth to life, nurtured and sustained life, and sent it forth into the world to work to bring about change, hope filled, positive change for all who inhabited it. They are our ancestors, our foremothers, our "sheroes," and we stand on their shoulders and in the shoes they made for us. They knew what needed to be done and did it, and so can we. They knew when the time was right to fight and when it was right to "hunker down" with arms spread wide around children and family, and so do we. They help us to understand how we got here and show us the way forward. The named and unnamed women of the Bible provide us with a vision of renewed life in spite of and despite all of the obstacles this world lays before us. Without them, we would not be.

Womanist Theology and Spirituality

These new methods of interpreting sacred scripture are a product of the theological shifts that took place in the latter half of the twentieth century. Men and women of all races and creeds began to demand a freedom long withheld by the dominant societies in which they lived. As noted in the previous chapter, in the United States the Civil Rights movement stirred up long-held resentments and frustrations, serving as a catalyst for liberation movements across the globe while itself being influenced by them. The impetus for civil and human rights could be said to be the actions of the Holy Spirit inspiring countless numbers to stand up and demand their liberation. Black women, although often overlooked, were a critical part of the Civil Rights movement. From the Montgomery bus boycott through the sit-ins and freedom rides, the freedom summer voting schools, and the many nonviolent marches and demonstrations, women were active and engaged participants. A Black folk saying notes: "If Rosa Parks had not sat down, Martin Luther King Jr. could not have stood up." Black women stood, prayed, marched, sat-in, bussed, and in all ways imaginable worked together with Black men to bring about equality.

It is only with the increased number of women gaining college degrees and beginning to mine their and their mother's and grandmother's experiences in the United States that we are finally beginning to hear the voices of Black women telling the stories of their lives. Much of this can be attributed to the emergence of womanist theology, a theology of, by, and for Black women that emerged in the latter part of the 1980s in direct response to the publication of *In Search of Our Mothers' Gardens: Womanist Essays*, a collection by Alice Walker that brought the term *womanist* to public notice.[23] Walker initiated the womanist movement by adding a detailed four-part definition of the term to her collection of essays.[24] Many Black women took up this term and its four-pronged definition by Walker as a foundation for speaking the truths of their lives as Black women.

By this time Black theology had been actively engaged in church and academia for more than a decade, but the young women studying under Black male theologians noticed a gaping hole in their methodology—the absence of Black women's voices and experience. It was as if Black women had not existed during slavery, Reconstruction, or the civil rights, Black Power, and Black Nationalism movements. Mining and retrieving that history became the goal of womanist theologians, initially Black Christian women, but over time expanding into the secular world of historians and others as well as into other religious realms such as Islam. As a womanist, I am in agreement with my womanist sisters in acknowledging that African American women must use "the 'stuff' of women's lives to spin a narrative of their persistent effort to rise above and beyond those persons and situations, which attempt to hold them down." Our sources are social, political, anthropological, and, especially, literary, because we see "Black women's literary tradition 'as a valid source for the central rubrics of the Black woman's odyssey' for it is in her literary writings that she sets forth the documentation of the living out of Black lives in a world confronted daily by racism, sexism, and poverty."[25]

Critiquing feminist theology for its overemphasis on gender, and Black theology for its masculine perspective, womanists sought to develop a theological perspective that spoke to the multiple oppression of Black women due to race, class, and gender. They asserted that these issues had to be dealt with as a unity and not separately because they affected the lives of African American women in a tri-dimensional way.

As with other liberation theologies, womanists sought to answer questions about their faith and praxis that emerged from their own lives. They asked: Who is Jesus for a Black woman today? What is the significance of his life, death, and resurrection? As discussed above, they scrutinized the Bible for stories of women that were applicable to their present-day lives and found especially relevant those of Hagar and Mary Magdalene. They explored African American history to recover the voices of women such as Harriet Tubman, Linda Brent, and Sojourner Truth as well as contemporaries such as Rosa Parks, Fannie Lou Hamer, Septima Clark, and Elsa

Barker, women whose participation had furthered the cause of African Americans but whose contributions had too often been sidelined or ignored.

The first generation of womanist theologians included Jacquelyn Grant, Delores S. Williams, Katie Cannon, Kelly Brown Douglas, and Emilie Townes, among others. They were all Protestant, and several had studied under James H. Cone. Cannon, one of the first to publish, explored the life and works of author and anthropologist Zora Neale Hurston in order to "engage the matrix of virtues which emerge from the real-lived texture of the Black community."[26] As an ethicist, Cannon raised questions regarding the moral situation of Black women in today's world and the triple jeopardy in which they find themselves. As noted before, Williams explored the story of Hagar as a source for African American women's ability to survive in wilderness situations, asserting that survival must come before liberation and that Jesus modeled that survival tradition by his life of resistance. She negatively critiques atonement theology for its overemphasis on surrogacy, an overemphasis that has forced women, especially Black women, into positions of surrogacy that have restricted their lives and freedoms and sometimes cost them their lives.[27]

Both Grant and Douglas discuss the christological significance of Jesus for Black women and the Black community. As with Black male theologians, Grant argues that the "social context for Black Christology is the black experience of oppression and the struggle against it."[28] For Black women, this means recognizing their triple (and quadruple) jeopardy as women, women of color, and women historically on the lowest rung of the economic ladder (a fourth aspect, that of sexual orientation, was not initially acknowledged even by womanists). Grant acknowledges the negative impact of these forms of oppression on the entire Black community, male and female. For Black women, Jesus is one with them, the divine co-sufferer who empowers and saves Blacks in situations of oppression, an understanding grounded in God's direct revelation to them as Black women, as revealed and witnessed to in sacred scripture and in their historical experience. God/ Jesus is creator, sustainer of life, comforter, and liberator. God becomes concrete not only in the man Jesus, for he was crucified, but also in the lives of those who will accept the challenges of the risen Savior—the Christ.[29]

Kelly Brown Douglas questions the absence of women's voices and experience historically and theologically. She presents both a sociopolitical and religio-cultural analysis that confronts racism, classism, sexism, and heterosexism, and lifts up aspects of Black life that sustain and nurture survival and liberation. She asserts that a "spirituality of resistance" resides in Black women that empowers their survival and, like Grant, sees no significance in Jesus' maleness but rather emphasizes the multidimensional aspect of women's oppression and the need to focus on survival and liberation for all in the Black community. Christ is "sustainer, liberator, and prophet" in the face of the hegemonic oppressions confronting Black women. For both Douglas and Grant, Christ, when acting on the side of the oppressed, is a "black woman."[30]

Delores Williams brings a radically different approach to Black Christology by negating the significance of liberation as the most critical aspect of Christ's message; rather, survival is what is most important. She asks: What value does liberation have for a destroyed people? Williams grounds her Christology on the wilderness experience of Black women who have been instrumental in providing for the survival of the community yet have historically received little recognition. This wilderness experience can be traced in the story of Hagar, who not only survived but communicated with God in her own right and became the head of a people.

New generations of Black and womanist theologians continue to respond to the question of who Jesus is for twenty-first-century African Americans. The voices of gay/lesbian/transgendered/queer African Americans are being integrated into both theologies, challenging the male and heterosexual limitations historically placed on them. JoAnne Terrell critiques early womanists for their lack of inclusivity while affirming that "the cross is about God's love for humankind." Those who suffer can be redeemed because of God's "with-us-ness," which means we are "already-at-one" with God.[31]

Other womanists have sought to construct womanist spiritualities that speak of and to the resources that Black women have mined in their efforts to not only survive but build viable, vibrant Black communities. Emilie Townes sees womanist spirituality as "a social witness . . . born out of a people's struggle and determination to continue to find ways to answer the question, Do you want to be healed? With the Yes! of our lives and the work we do for justice." Townes continues:

> Womanist spirituality is not grounded in the notion that spirituality is a force, a practice separate from who we are moment by moment. It is the deep kneading of humanity and divinity into one breath, one hope, and one vision. Womanist spirituality is not only a way of living, it is a style of witness that seeks to cross the yawning chasm of hatreds and prejudices and oppressions into a deeper and richer love of God as we experience Jesus in our lives. This love extends to self and others. It holds together the individual and the community in a soulful relationship that cannot dwell more on one than the other partner of the relation but holds both in the same frame.
>
> Womanist spirituality is the working out of what it means for each of us to seek compassion, justice, worship, and devotion in our witness. This understanding of spirituality seeks to grow into wholeness of spirit and body, mind and heart —- into holiness in God.[32]

Affirming that this spirituality is rooted "in the moral wisdom of African American women,"[33] Townes explores this wisdom as it is found in literature and autobiography, in poetry and sermons created by Black women, revealing how the Spirit has been the source and sustainer for the witness of African American women to this very day.

Kelly Brown Douglas reflects on spirituality by exploring the Black body and Christianity's role in both humanizing and dehumanizing it:

> Authentic spirituality—that is, a relationship to divine reality—was not a matter of the mind [for enslaved blacks]; it was rather a matter of the soul and body. This meant, then, that a person's spiritual condition—that is, the state of one's soul—and/or one's immediate relationship to divinity should be empirically evident through some form of bodily expression. That the body was considered a means by which "divinity" could manifest itself implied that the body had sacral value. In other words, the body was a potential vehicle for divine witness.[34]

She argues that African American spirituality, therefore, is a spirituality of resistance:

> Historically a *spirituality of resistance* has been central to black people's survival and wholeness in a society that demeans their very black humanity. Such spirituality is characterized by a sense of connection to one's heritage as well as to the divine. As such, it provided black men and women with a buffer of defense against white cultural characterizations of them as beings unworthy of freedom, dignity, even life. At the same time, a spirituality of resistance grants them, especially black women, a sense of control over their own bodies. For just as it connects them to their God and to a cultural history, it also affirms the sacred value of their bodies. And in so doing, a spirituality of resistance has uniquely empowered black women to claim agency over their sexuality.[35]

She admits however that this spiritual resolve often is not enough; it does not always translate into actual physical agency. Black women saw their bodies and souls as intimately connected because it connected them with God. Therefore, a loss of agency also impacted negatively their very souls: "The very spirituality that was key to their resistance and positive sense of self became potentially damning when their efforts to resist the sexual violence of white men failed. Hence, they were left to experience an almost impenetrable sense of shame. For not only had black women's bodies been violated but so too had their souls," thereby disrupting their relationship with God.[36] This Douglas sees as the result of a Platonized theology that sees things of the flesh, especially sexuality, as evil and harmful to one's relationship with God and to one's soul. The resulting sense of shame has negatively influenced how Blacks see themselves, especially their bodies, and is an issue of growing concern in today's "rap/hip-hop"–oriented world where women are often depicted only as sexualized bodies.

Flora Wilson Bridges explores African American spirituality as "a spiritual matrix," one "that helped African Americans to forge their own world-view":

> African American spirituality was the "sorcerer's stone" upon which black people in America birthed and nurtured a new-old culture: they created a new kinship network, raised and socialized children in their own way, built a new-old religion, and continued creatively and effectively to articulate and struggle to achieve their high hopes and dreams in the face of the horrifying and spirit-numbing conditions of American racism.[37]

Bridges's four themes of "a unified world-view, black people's self-definition of human identity, spirituality embodied as the call to protest, and the quest for community,"[38] all undergirded by the motif of freedom, correlate to the ways in which African American spirituality has been presented here. Bridges concludes by formulating a definition of African American spirituality with two characteristics: the first is "a cultural resilience or the ability to bounce or spring back into shape or position after being stretched, bent or compressed by cultural oppression," and the second is the "effects" of that resilience as it defines African American values and cultural expression in the people's quest for identity and the building of community.[39] As with other womanists, she grounds her theologizing in the actual lives and histories of Black men and women in the United States who personify the spirituality she has formulated through their witness:

> The African-American community expresses itself spiritually and religiously through a basically collective self-understanding that values and evaluates everything in terms of its capability to inspire loyalty to the community's primary concern of survival with human dignity and self-determination. African-American spirituality is the foundation of the embodied soul's ability to be centered or anchored in God and then stand for God in the community. When the individual stands in community, he or she simultaneously stands in the presence of the Source of ultimate meaning.[40]

Finally, in her work, *Enfleshing Freedom*,[41] M. Shawn Copeland, a Black Catholic theologian, discusses the critical significance of embodiment for womanist theologians. She has described how slavery sought to deface God's image and likeness in Black humanity and thereby "debase blacks being-in-*communion* with creation." Copeland maintains that the created spirit is enfleshed "through the struggle to achieve and exercise freedom in history and society." Thus, "the black body" becomes "a site of divine revelation and, thus, is a 'basic human sacrament.'"

She also describes the body as "the medium through which the person, as essential freedom, achieves and realizes selfhood through communion with other embodied selves."[42] Thus, for Copeland, the spirituality of Black people is an "embodied spirituality" that reclaims our understanding of eros in ways that go far beyond terms of sex and sexuality:

Eros as embodied spirituality suffuses and sustains depth or value-laden experiences and relationships that emerge whenever" we share[e] deeply any pursuit [whether] physical, emotional, psychic, or intellectual with another person."[43] Eros enhances our capacity for joy and knowledge, honors and prompts our deepest yearnings for truth and life, and validates our refusal of docility and submission in the face of oppression. Eros steadies us as we reach out to other bodies in reverence, passion, and compassion, resisting every temptation to use or assimilate the other and the Other for our own self-gratification, purpose, or plan Eros empowers and affirms life.[44]

In Copeland's view the spirituality of Black Americans, and in particular African American women, is one "that empowers and affirms life." It is a spirituality that enables them to become and to be the fullness of *imago Dei*.

As the third and fourth generations of womanist theologians emerge and as Black women continue to dig deep and speak the truth for all, we are sure to see even more developed discussions of African American spirituality. The womanists discussed above, and all womanists, reveal the depth and breadth of womanist theological reflection and the impact Black women have had and continue to have. They continue to tell the "old, old story" in inclusive and provocative ways.

African American Catholic Women

As related in earlier chapters, the history of the Catholic Africans who came as early as the sixteenth century to the Americas is not as well known as that of those who arrived in the colonies along the eastern part of North America. But there is an older history, one that traces back to the early church in Africa and in the Spanish and French colonies of the Southwest and Louisiana. It is in these records of baptisms, marriages, and confraternities that we learn of Spanish-speaking and French-speaking Catholic Africans who helped to lay the foundation for the Roman Catholic Church in the United States. In these records we discover the voices of Black Catholic women who, like their Protestant sisters, were often ignored or overlooked when the official histories were written. But they were the ones who gave birth to that history, quite literally, and who sustained and nurtured it for generations, building the thriving Black Catholic community of today. Many of their names and stories are lost to us, but others are finally being brought to light so we can see how the path was laid.

Some of the earliest references to Black Catholics can be found in old baptismal records dating back to the sixteenth century in churches founded by Spanish-speaking and French-speaking persons of African descent who, with their European co-religionists, kept a meticulous record of births, deaths, baptisms, and marriages. In the oldest U.S. city, St. Augustine, Florida, founded in 1565, we find "the oldest ecclesiastical documents for the United States." Blacks are mentioned in all of them "as having been baptized and married" just like everyone else.[45] Detailed records can also be found for the City of Los Angeles, founded in 1781 by twelve Catholic families, only two of which were white or European. These records provide us with a rich history of the earliest period of Black women's presence in the colonies that were, over time, to become the United States of America.

The Catholic Church in the South (especially in Louisiana due to the presence of people of free colored status) was often helpful in aiding and encouraging free women of color in their efforts. Although the church had supported slavery for centuries and arguably was the cause of its introduction into the Americas, those in Rome slowly came to realize the inherent sinfulness of slavery, especially with its brutal dehumanization in the Americas. Paradoxically, the institutional Catholic Church became, in many ways, the moral protector of many of these women and helped to educate them at a time when most white Southern women were still uneducated. They were taught the skills of reading, writing, ciphering, and sewing by the church, which, at the same time, imparted religious doctrine that reinforced what their mothers and grandmothers had told them about the social roles of women.[46] These skills and resourcefulness were to serve them well in the years to come, especially in overcoming the racism and sexism that persisted within the Catholic hierarchy and its members.

By founding Black women's religious orders, the Oblates of Providence (1829) and the Sisters of the Holy Family (1851), Mother Elizabeth Lange and Mother Henriette de Lille were instrumental in helping to build and preserve the Black Catholic community. Both acted courageously on their personal desires to serve God and their fellow Black Catholics. They deemed it necessary to reject the roles usually reserved for free women of color in American society, roles as either domestics and laborers (in Baltimore) or concubines (in New Orleans) and to seek ways in which they could help to strengthen African Americans both in their faith and in their self-understanding. Historian Cyprian Davis observes:

> In a time when black people were accorded little or no respect or esteem, in a time when black women were degraded by slaveholders or abused by white employers, in a society where black women were considered to be weak in morality, black sisters were a counter sign and a proof that the black Catholic community was rooted in faith and devotion; for vocations arise from a faith-filled people.[47]

At a time when no white religious order would accept women of African descent, Elizabeth Lange and Henriette De Lille and their sisters in the faith persisted in their efforts to develop religious institutions to provide education in the basics of reading, writing, and arithmetic but also in skills such as sewing and cooking. They believed that by so doing, young Black women would "hopefully be prepared to move from lives of domestic drudgery, which was the fate of most Black women, free or slave, into higher callings, including the religious life."[48]

Joseph Brown describes these early Black religious women:

> For them a life of *consecrated virginity* was emancipation from the demonization of their sexuality, and their choices were public acts, confronting the worlds into which they were born, and from which they daily fled. . . .
>
> Without their religious garb [which they were not allowed to wear publicly until after the Civil War] and their ascetic language, these women would be looked upon as the first African-American business and professional women, the precursors of the women entrepreneurs of the Far West and the urban East of the late nineteenth and early twentieth centuries. In many places, these black women religious built long-lasting institutions of education, benevolence, and social development that are the Catholic equivalents of the great institutions created by the black Protestant churches.[49]

Despite obstacles at every turn, despite the denial of their right to participate in the sacraments of the church on an equal basis, despite being denied recognition for their ongoing presence and contributions to the church in the United States, African American Catholic women did not allow anyone to stop them in the practice of their faith and its implementation in their communities. Convinced that God was a God of justice in whose image they too had been created, they persevered in spreading the good news of Jesus Christ far and wide and inspired countless others to follow them. They "found critical ways in which to mold their worlds, to create their identities, and to influence the worlds and identities of those around them."[50] They were self-motivated and self-empowered, sustained by the Holy Spirit, and they refused to let anyone or anything stand in their way.

Black Catholic women, as all women, held their families together, instructed their children, and fought against every form of injustice. Black religious women, despite being ignored and denigrated in the church, were instrumental in maintaining and growing the Black community. As religious, they often had greater freedoms than the laity to challenge the hierarchy in its stance toward Black Catholics. They taught in parochial schools nationwide to Catholic and unchurched students, who often became members of the church as a result of their holiness and zeal. They passed on the values and traditions of their people and their faith and the teachings of their beloved church.

In the aftermath of the Second Vatican Council, Black Catholic women formed lay and religious organizations that encouraged an opening to the world. Many were involved in the Civil Rights movement, such as Diane Nash, one of the founders of the Student Non-Violent Coordinating Committee.[51] Others worked within the Catholic Church itself to open doors for Black men and women to take on leadership roles. Their spirituality was one of resilience and resistance rooted in the sacraments that sustained and nurtured them. They called for more Black priests and religious, but also for more Black bishops as heads of dioceses, and they began to develop liturgies that brought forth the gifts they shared with all persons of African descent to share them with the church as a whole.

Some Black Catholic women, like Sr. Thea Bowman, inspired others with their lives of courage and resilience, reteaching the songs and prayers Black mothers had taught for years; others sought to share the history and values of Black Catholics from Africa and the Americas to inspire those forging new ways of being Catholic in the twentieth century. They modeled their lives on Jesus and his mother whose quiet courage and resilience gave them encouragement on their journey. They also reconnected with those saints of the church whom they knew to be of African ancestry, such as St. Martin de

Porres, St. Benedict the Black, St. Augustine, and Sts. Perpetua and Felicity, among countless others restored to renewed life within their communities.

Today, Black Catholic scholars are developing Black and womanist theologies out of their experiences in the Roman Catholic Church as a means of acknowledging and affirming the authenticity of both their blackness and their Catholicity.[52]

Strong Women Keep a'Comin'

Black women, Protestant and Catholic alike, have been nurtured and sustained by a spirituality that paved the way for us and softened the rough places just enough for us to continue. As an African people we recognized the importance of and maintained our ties with the spiritual. In *Body and Soul: The Black Woman's Guide to Physical Health and Emotional Well-Being*, Linda Villarose affirms the importance of spirituality:

> Spirituality is a rock to hang on to when the world is rushing out of control. It is the unseen force that gives you the courage to push when you'd much rather pull. It shows the way when it seems there is no way. It makes sense out of the nonsense and encourages you to have faith—help is just around the corner.
>
> It is the balm that soothes and heals your inner wounds. With spirituality, you rest easy knowing that whatever aids you, enrages you, troubles you, or gets on your last nerve, this too shall pass. It's the map to inner peace on a road that never ends.[53]

Black women remain the "heartbeat" of our African American communities, a status for which they are both exalted and maligned. Black women have the potential to create a community of faith that acts collectively to transform our world. When we heal the woundedness inside us, we make ourselves ready to enter more fully into community. We can experience the totality of life because we have become fully life-affirming. Like our ancestors, using our powers to the fullest, we share the secrets of healing and come to know sustained joy.

The women of scripture discussed above—Eve, Hagar, Mary of Magdala, and Mary, the mother of God—are only a few of the women in sacred scripture who speak words of womanist wisdom and dare to become other than what they have been told they should be. Like their Black sisters, they had borne the burden of rape and forced sterilization and their children were sold away or taken away by the state. They may have also lost their names, their history, their family, and all that makes up a human life, yet these women have been held in God's hand and named by God. For to be a woman named by God, to be a woman called into God's service, is to be a woman who can change the surrounding world. These sisters in solidarity speak words of Black wisdom and live lives of hope, courage, and faith, even in a world that may see them as nothing.

8

We Who Believe in Freedom

Spirituality in Action

*We have been believers believing in the black
gods of an old land, . . .*

*And in the white gods of a new land we have
been believers. . . .*

*We have been believers yielding substance for
the world.*
*With our hands have we fed a people and
out of our strength have they wrung the
necessities of a nation. Our song has filled
the twilight and our hope has heralded the
dawn.*

—Margaret Walker[1]

African American spirituality was forged in a fiery furnace,
one that shaped and molded a disparate people, Africans of
many nations and tribes, languages and traditions, beliefs and
cultures, into a single people—African Americans. They survived being torn from all that was familiar and then flung into
a cauldron of discrimination and prejudice. They withstood
torture, deprivation, hunger and thirst, winter's cold and summer's heat to become a Spirit-filled people who refused to let
themselves be beaten into the ground. Over centuries, buoyed

169

up by faith in a God who was intolerant of injustice and demanded the liberation of all of humanity, they grew strong and stepped forth in demand of their freedom. They believed their God would help them attain freedom and, though it may not have come as quickly or easily as they would have hoped, when freedom did eventually come they rejoiced in it.

For the most part, African Americans still remain a Spirit-filled people, yet over the centuries of bondage and oppression, even as they were being forged into this new people, there were always those who followed different gods or no gods, those who found different paths for expressing their faith in the one Christian God, and those who completely fell away from institutionalized religion. Nonetheless, they still had deeply embedded within them that Spirit that had sustained and nurtured their ancestors, and they sang and proclaimed that Spirit in religious and nonreligious ways. These alternate spiritualities are all a part of, even while apart from, the fullness of African American spirituality as expressed in the Christian tradition.

There are many different voices today articulating African American spirituality from particular perspectives. This concluding chapter highlights some of these perspectives while recognizing that African American spirituality is still a work in progress as new generations continue to look toward other paths or seek to redefine the "old, old story" passed down from their ancestors.

Womanist spiritualities, discussed in Chapter 7, continue to develop as we now enter the third and fourth wave of womanist theology in the United States. African American women speak from the core of their being about their relationship with God, with the men and women they love, and with their sisters, friends, and children in the Black community. Theirs is, as noted, a spirituality of resistance that has enabled Black women to carve out roles for themselves and those coming after them to build a strong and firm foundation of love, compassion, and faith in community.

Black male theologians and public intellectuals also have been vocal in defining and delineating the spirituality of African Americans, varying in language and tone, but all basically recognizing the same historical origins and many of the same threads. Like womanist theologians, they look ahead to what the future may bring as the Black community finds itself yet again in danger of dissolution from forces within and without its boundaries.

As they have finally begun to achieve a certain success and status in American society that is long overdue, many new challenges have arisen. Some have moved away from the institutional churches, no longer feeling the need for faith or to pursue other spiritualities, including those that promise wealth and prosperity but lose sight of the importance of family and community. Others, left behind in derelict urban ghettos, have fallen victim to despair and find solace in an "otherworldly escapist form of God or have abandoned religion entirely, looking only to themselves."[2] God is still present in the Black community and actively helping Blacks to reclaim and renew their faith and their spirituality. God hears their cries and responds to these new challenges by revealing to them new ways to be faithful, encouraging them to reach out, once again to those most in need. Theirs is still a spirituality of resistance, of survival, and of liberation.

Walter Earl Fluker:
Spirituality as a Basis for Ethical Leadership

Walter Earl Fluker, a professor of ethics at Boston University, notes that spirituality "refers to a way or ways of seeking or being in relationship with the other who is believed to be worthy of reverence and highest devotion." He sees the other as "intimately related to who I am and who I become."[3] The face of the other can be encountered in daily life and also in its transcendence and strangeness; it calls upon us to be fully human and ethical by confronting and acknowledging the other within our midst.

Fluker also describes spirituality as a "discipline that places emphasis on practice—spirituality is something that we do." He identifies three perspectives from which spirituality can be viewed, perspectives that we will see echoed and exemplified by others as well.

- Formal notions of spirituality that are related to established religions;
- Informal notions of spirituality that are "self-actualized" or self-defined by individuals or small groups that may or may not be associated with an established religious institution; and
- Philosophical or ethical notions of spirituality related to values and perceived goods (e.g., truth, beauty, justice, etc.).[4]

Formal notions of spirituality, that is, those grounded in the doctrine and rituals of a particular church or religion, are to be found within established religious institutions, Christian and non-Christian. Historically, African Americans have not placed great significance on these forms, but beginning with the development and growth of Black theologies of liberation, including womanist theology, more authors are looking at the more formal structures of spirituality, including liturgy, ritual, and other inherited practices that have persisted in the life of Black churches. Writers in this area include theologians Jamie Phelps, who explores the ecclesiology of the Catholic Church and its relationship to Black Catholics, and Gayraud Wilmore, who explores the Black church through the lens of Black historical experience stretching back to Africa and, in particular, the role and relationship of the Presbyterian Church to Black America.

Less formal notions of spirituality are becoming increasingly popular both within and outside the Black churches as well as globally. They cross religious denominations and often weave aspects of various faiths into a new spirituality or even renounce institutional religions in their entirety. They call for greater involvement with the environment or speak in terms of the goddess rather than God or see themselves as post-Christian, having moved beyond that religion's limitations and restrictions. Fluker acknowledges African American women writers, theologians, and preachers as examples of these understandings, including Iyanla Vanzant, Alice Walker, Oprah Winfrey, and many others.

At the same time, many young people under the age of thirty have adopted this approach in a very unstructured way, declaring themselves spiritual but not religious and proclaiming a spirituality that, ironically, places themselves at the center. They confess a personal relationship with a personal God that too often, however, seems to be made in their own image and likeness instead of the other way around, resulting in a religion and spirituality of "me." They have moved into new or renewed religions as well, such as Wicca (which highlights the feminine and interaction with nature), "goddess" (also emphasizes the feminine aspect), and new forms of paganism. At another level an increasing number of Black women in the United States have become practicing Buddhists, with some seeing Buddhism simply as a form of meditation but most as a religious belief that is often coupled with various forms of Christianity.[5]

In the third area of broader philosophical and ethical notions of spirit, Fluker notes that "spirituality is discussed as a source of authority for private and public discourse . . . located across the spectrum of conservative, liberal and progressive ideologies."[6] The African American writers he notes include Robert M. Franklin, Peter J. Paris, and Stephen L. Carter, as well as Sarah Lawrence-Lightfoot and James M. Washington.

Fluker views spirituality as key for the development of ethical leaders because it demands that they "cultivate and nurture a *sense of self* that recognizes the interrelatedness of life or *a sense of community*." He sees spirituality as "the core of the inner and social lives of ethical leaders," to be used as a resource when making decisions that can lead to social and political transformation.[7] Such leaders are critical for today, he affirms, especially for African Americans challenged by the growing emphasis on and promotion of science, technology, and business:

> For historically marginalized peoples, the relationship of spirituality, ethics, and leadership is most urgent. With the long-range economic, political, and social costs of war, a troubled market economy and rapid advances (crusades) in technology, science, and global democracy, we now have the makings of a social anarchy that threatens the very foundations of our social purpose.[8]

He concludes: "*Who will go for us, and whom shall we send?*," questions of critical importance as we enter the second decade of the twenty-first century.[9]

James H. Evans, Jr.:
Spirituality and Social Transformation

James H. Evans, a professor of theology at Colgate Rochester Crozier Divinity School, defines African American spirituality as "the quest for communion with God as God is known both within and outside of ourselves. Spirituality or spiritualities are funded by our understanding of the divine spirit and the human spirit."[10] But for him, spirituality is not simply about forms of prayer and reflection; rather, Evans views spirituality in terms of social transformation. Noting that spirituality has often been related to the political order, he writes:

> Liberation spirituality is, therefore, a political spirituality—this point should not be concealed—and it is concerned and involved with material things like bread,

clothing, health, and shelter. In this sense liberation
spirituality is "materialistic." However, it is in these
material things that this spirituality primarily encounters
Jesus, the Jesus who is the person in need. . . . With one
stroke, liberation spirituality unites love for God and
love for neighbor, this life and the next, the "material"
world and the "spiritual" world.[11]

Evans calls for a "spirituality for new life" that recognizes
"that authentic liberation from the forces of sin and death
requires both personal spiritual renewal and public social
transformation."[12] Such a spirituality would view human
work as a positive force for transforming the social order
and affirm that "the work of renewal and transformation is
inseparable from the quest for survival, liberation and wholeness" as is seen most particularly in womanist spirituality. He
quotes Yvonne Patricia Chireau, who recognizes that

the spiritual lives of Black People in the United States
have historically extended beyond church, beyond
mosque and temple, spilling over into mundane aspects
of living and into daily existence. Transcending institutional expression, African American spirituality has
flourished outside of sectarian boundaries, permeating
the private sphere and the public realm, filling the spaces
where everyday needs are considered and met.[13]

For Evans, this spirituality affirms that "renewal and transformation are the work of the Holy Spirit in the world."

The Holy Spirit is that power which continually renews
life, animates human history, and validates the cosmos
confirming the beauty and aptness of God's initial
design. The resurrection proclaims the transformation
of the created order, calling it forward to a new hope
and life in God. The Holy Spirit is that power which
continually transforms life, directs human history, and

guides the cosmos, confirming the passion and care of God.[14]

In many ways Evans's understanding of spirituality is very much akin to that of Martin Luther King Jr., as discussed earlier. Spirituality and the political order are seen to be intimately connected and interactive, calling forth a practical response from African Americans to work to transform society on behalf of the "least among us."

Peter J. Paris: Spirituality of a People

The focus of Peter J. Paris, an ordained Baptist minister and a professor emeritus of social ethics at Princeton Theological Seminary, is on the spirituality of African peoples in Africa and the Diaspora.[15] He explores the religious and moral values of traditional African religious worldviews, showing that these values have been retained even though modified in African American theological and spiritual reflection. His understanding of spirituality is that it is embodied; it is connected to the dynamic and social movement of life. Thus, for Paris, "the spirituality of a people refers to the animating and integrative power that constitutes the principal frame of meaning for individual and collective experiences. Metaphorically, the spirituality of a people is synonymous with the soul of a people: the integrating center of their power and meaning." The movement of life, he argues, has survival as its goal but also the "union of those forces of life that have the power either to threaten or destroy life on the one hand, or to preserve and enhance it, on the other hand."[16]

In seeking to formulate a theory of social ethics, Paris makes the following arguments. First, "African peoples both on the continent and in the Diaspora are diverse in cultural form yet united in their underlying spirituality," as is evidenced by the different languages and cultural conventions that make up the fundamental values of any particular group. He calls this the "unity in diversity" of African spirituality. Second, he affirms "that the realities of cultural diversity and the unity of African spirituality both separate and unite African and African American religious and moral traditions." Lastly, Paris asserts "that a dynamic principle of unity permeates the diversity of African cultural traditions" in Africa and the Diaspora. The result is the bringing to life of the understanding of "I am because we are" or unity in diversity.[17]

Paris's vision of the moral life relies on four concepts: the realm of the spirit, the realm of the community, the realm of the family, and the realm of the individual person who seeks to integrate these realms within him or herself.[18] The result, once again, is unity in diversity. That unity calls upon individuals to act in community to right the wrongs of human society. To be morally virtuous one must do what is best for one's community, and community means being in right relationship to the realms of spirit, tribe, and family.

Where Evans can be seen to be developing a spirituality that fits the formal notions categorized by Fluker, Paris's work, while integrating formal notions, most clearly relates to ethical notions of spirituality. His writings relate to the values that emerge from a spirituality grounded in the culture, faith, and history of African peoples, both in Africa and the Diaspora.

Carlyle Fielding Stewart III: Soul Survivors

African Americans are soul survivors according to Carlyle Fielding Stewart III, senior pastor of Hope United Methodist Church in Southfield, Michigan.[19] They are soul survivors "because African American spirituality has enabled them to adapt, transcend, and transform the absurdities of racism, oppression, and adverse human conditions into a creative soul culture that has helped them to maintain sanity, vitality, and wholeness." An "ethos" has been created "where creative and resistant soul force has compelled black Americans to creatively and consistently face and overcome their plight."[20]

Stewart defines spirituality as

> the full matrix of beliefs, power, values, and behaviors that shape people's consciousness, understanding, and capacity of themselves in relation to divine reality. Spirituality is also a process by which people interpret, disclose, formulate, adapt, and innovate reality and their understandings of God within a specific context or culture.[21]

Two critical elements of Stewart's understanding of spirituality are creative soul force and resistant soul force. The former "is the spirit of creativity that forges and fosters culture as a means of constructing and transforming reality." It enables African Americans to "adapt, transform, and transcend reality." The latter "is the power that thwarts the complete domestication of the spirit for purposes of subjugation, domination, and annihilation." It is the power "to create, transform and transcend those barriers and constraints that enforce complete domestication" and the devaluation of human [Black] life.[22]

Acknowledging that there can be many varieties and definitions of spirituality, as we have seen, Stewart presents five statements that develop his understanding of spirituality:

- God, as creator of the spiritual life force is the cohesive nexus of black experience. God is the creative, animative, integrative, and transformative center of all being and existence. He is the source of spirituality;

- African American spirituality is a socially functional process or praxis that creates an ethos and culture by which black people encounter, interpret, adopt, adapt, integrate, transform, and transcend human experience through the creative appropriation of divine spirit for self-empowerment and survival;

- It is a creative process and practice. Its functions are formative, unitive or integrative, corroborative, transformative, and sacralative or consecrative and they, in turn, constitute African American Spirituality as a paradigm for human freedom;
- The by-products of African American Spirituality are creativity, adaptation, ritualization, innovation, improvisation, transcendence, and transformation as can especially be seen in African American music, prayer, and preaching;
- African American Spirituality and African American culture in dialogue create a matrix of practices and beliefs that informs, inspires, reforms, and transforms the meaning, value, and purpose of African American existence.[23]

African American spirituality is critically important for the formation of human consciousness that "functions primarily as an intrinsic, interior psychospiritual cultural force within the very fibers and corpuscles of black being, soul, and consciousness." It has thus enabled Blacks' accommodation and adaptation to dominant society and culture while resisting complete assimilation and annihilation.[24] "The African-American church as the primary institution preserving the creation, perpetuation, and practice of black spirituality . . . has engendered the development of spiritual practices that invariably insulate blacks from complete subjugation and dehumanization by the larger culture."[25]

Thus, Stewart's sociopolitical understanding of Black spirituality provides a model of human freedom because of its role in shaping Black consciousness and in empowering the birth and development of Black community.

Cornel West: Combative Spirituality

Cornel West, a public intellectual and philosopher based at Princeton University, remains rooted in his upbringing in the Black Baptist tradition. Thus, although not a cleric and more inclined toward Marxist philosophy, he understands the critical nature and validity of the Black church in the Black community. In many of his works he speaks of a combative spirituality as

> a form of spirituality—of community and communion—that preserves meaning by fighting against the bombardments of claims that we are inferior or deficient. Combative spirituality sustains persons in their humanity but also transcends solely the political. It embraces a political struggle, but it also deals with issues of death or dread, of despair or disappointment. . . . A combative spirituality accents a political struggle but goes beyond it by looking death and dread and despair and disappointment and disease in the face and saying that there is in fact a hope beyond these.[26]

This is not, West emphasizes, a deferred hope but one that "calls into question all illusions that there'll be Utopia around the corner."[27] Such a hope requires the stamina of a long-distance runner rather than the desire for a quick fix that is so much a part of U.S. culture today. Combative spirituality is rooted in a subversive joy,

> the ability to transform tears into laughter, a laughter that allows one to acknowledge just how difficult the journey is, but to also acknowledge one's own sense of humanity and folly and humor in the midst of this very serious struggle. It's a joy that allows one both a space, a distance from the absurd, but also empowers one to engage back in the struggle when the time is necessary.[28]

Combative spirituality is the third part of a three-pronged analysis of the African resources to be found in Black spirituality. The others are kinetic orality, which expresses itself in song, prayer, and preaching, and a passionate physicality that emphasizes Black control and power over events and forces affecting the Black community. As West affirms:

> This stress on the performative and the pragmatic, on pageantry and the histrionic put a premium on prospective moral practice as forward looking ethical struggle for Black parishioners. This sense of struggle paradoxically cultivated a historical patience and subversive joy, a sober survival ethic and an openness to seize credible liberation opportunities.[29]

West's philosophical approach to African American spirituality broadens our understanding while at the same time reinforcing what we have come to know, that African American spirituality engages Black people at the very core of their being and orients them toward practical action in the world and not apart from it.

Gayraud S. Wilmore: Pragmatic Spirituality

Gayraud S. Wilmore, a Presbyterian minister and theologian, speaks of an Africentric pragmatic spirituality, one that focuses on the meaning and being of people of African descent. He is one of the earliest Black theologians to call for the mining and inclusion of African and African American history and culture as an ongoing source for Black theology. Wilmore employs an Africentric lens, in other words, a lens "that clarifies my perception of what, in this world, envelopes and conditions me as an *African* American," a descendant of African slaves, and as a follower of Jesus Christ.[30] He discusses the spiritual formation of a slave in the following way:

[The slaves developed] a hybrid form of spirituality that was more than the solipsistic practices of holiness, the concentration on the presence of God and the feeling of personal fulfillment that sometimes comes with it. The spirituality of the African slave conjoined the sacred and the profane; the intuitive and charismatic apprehension of an invisible spiritual world with the practical requirements of a visible physical world that, after more than six hundred years, continues to be oppressive and not infrequently brutal to people whose skin color is other than white.[31]

For Wilmore, African American spirituality is a pragmatic or practical spirituality because its emphasis is not solely on otherworldly aspirations but on everyday human considerations and consequences. It is a spirituality "rooted in its human direction and goal, its propensity for loving service to others as an emulation of God's love of humankind that is manifested primarily in the biblical picture of Jesus' earthly ministry to the 'least' of his sisters and brothers." Such a spirituality "focuses religion on the nitty-gritty problems and purposes of daily life." He continues:

Pragmatic spirituality is exemplified in the healing and liberating ministry of Jesus. It frees us to be human in a way that makes a palpable difference in others' lives. That is why Jesus, the Fixer, the Healer, the Liberating God, was at the center of black faith in the early African American churches and continues to be the same for most interpreters of black and womanist theologies today.[32]

Thus, Wilmore emphasizes the sociocultural aspect of the Black religious experience, yet at the same time insists on the pragmatic nature of that experience. This has led to his development of an understanding of African American spirituality that nurtures and sustains Blacks in their ordinary lives while enabling them to act on behalf of their eventual liberation.

Robert M. Franklin: A Diversity of Traditions

In *Another Day's Journey* Robert M. Franklin, a theologian/ethicist who is currently president of Morehouse College, describes seven spiritual traditions that he believes persist within the Black church:

- Evangelical: seeks deeper knowledge of God's word, following conversion, through study, teaching, and preaching;
- Holiness: seeks purity of life and thought through the disciplines of fasting, renunciation, and prayer;
- Charismatic: seeks empowerment through the Holy Spirit by tarrying in the search for spiritual gifts, and in prayer;
- Social justice: seeks public righteousness through community activism, political advocacy, and preaching;
- Afrocentric: seeks to celebrate the halcyon days of the African past and to affirm black identity in the present through cultural displays and identification with African history and rituals;
- Contemplative: seeks intimacy with God and employs the contemplative disciplines and meditation;
- New age: is nontheistic; seeks peace of mind and harmony with nature through meditation, chanting, and music.[33]

Arguably, these seven traditions are not always as clearly defined or as distinct from one another as Franklin presents them. As is often the case with African American traditions, they are all threads in a larger tapestry. There is a great deal of overlap and interchange, as can be seen, for example, in a contemporary Methodist church that emphasizes prayer (contemplation) and holiness (the "method" in Methodism), is Afrocentric, advocates social justice, and also supports the further education of its membership in scripture. Many Black churches tend to weave many of these threads together at different points in their existence.

Franklin also leaves out those Black Christians who are members of the Roman Catholic Church and who have woven yet another thread into the tapestry of African American spirituality. Their spirituality, a eucharistic and sacramental spirituality that seeks union with God through the Bread of Life who is Jesus Christ, is also contemplative, charismatic, and oriented toward social justice. Aspects of Black Catholicism partake also of the holiness tradition; fasting, prayer, and renunciation of sin are significant parts of Catholic life. Increasingly, Black Catholics have also begun to integrate aspects of Afrocentrism into their liturgical rituals as they seek to reclaim their African heritage and apply it to their daily lives.

Franklin's listing, however, provides a useful overview of the many forms that African American spirituality has taken and continues to take as African Americans continue to grow in self-understanding and in understanding their relationship with the Holy. Calling attention to these different categories raises different periods of the Black experience for review and examination in greater depth while helping us to realize the complex nature and yet utter simplicity of African American spirituality.

Bryan N. Massingale: Lamentation and Compassion

Writing from the perspective of a Roman Catholic ethicist, Massingale does not directly address Black spirituality.

However, his discussion of racial justice and the lack thereof in the Roman Catholic Church is grounded in Black Catholic spirituality. This can be seen especially in his discussion of the spirituals in his book, *Racial Justice and the Catholic Church*. He uses the language of compassion and lament to reveal how African Americans were able to withstand slavery and Jim Crow and remain a people united against their oppression.

Massingale defines lamentation as "an expression of complaint, grief, and hope rooted in a 'trust against trust' that God hears the cry of the afflicted and will respond compassionately to their need." Loss and hope coexist in a creative tension, as can be seen in many of the spirituals, creating a spirituality not of despair or despondency but of constantly renewed hope. For Massingale, "honest lament then gives rise to a deep sense of compassion."[34] Compassion is on a different level from lamentation. There is sorrow but also identification with another person, and action to help the other as best one can. Lamentation and compassion can thus be seen as the foundation of Black spirituality and a core element in the building up of Black community.

Massingale then directs this understanding toward the Catholic Church as a whole, calling for recognition of the oppressive situation in which Black Catholics still find themselves within the church and, more important, of the possibilities for meaningful practical action to establish cross-racial solidarity, action rooted in compassion.

The theologians, ethicists, and public intellectuals discussed above, like most African American Christians, also cross boundaries of the different traditions in many ways. What is of critical importance to affirm is that all of these traditions are legitimate expressions of African American spirituality, even though most Christians would not accept New Age spirituality because of its non-theistic foundation. Coupled with the spiritualities of womanist theologians (Chapter 7), the Black community finds itself immersed in the spirit of God, continuing to "lean on" God's everlasting arm of justice, righteousness, and love. The majority of African Americans in the twenty-first century are still Christian but with a sizeable number, especially in the years after the Civil Rights movement, of Muslims (orthodox Sunni and not Nation of Islam[35]), while a growing number have moved to Buddhism (especially Black women, as noted above) and other religious faiths, including the Yoruba tradition, Vodoun, Candomblé, and Santería.

Alternative Spiritualities

As the number of African immigrants entering the United States continues to grow, it is conceivable that African American spirituality will weave in new threads from contemporary forms of African traditional religions, African Christianity, and African Islam as well as from the African Caribbean Catholic religions being imported to the United States by immigrants from Haiti, Brazil, Cuba, Puerto Rico, and other areas. Further research needs to be done on the impact these newcomers are having on African American Christianity as well as on African American lives. Over time, they will probably be absorbed in part and rejected in part as African Americans continue to reflect on their ongoing relationship with a God of love and justice who has guided them "this far on their way."[36]

One significant change noted at the outset of this work is the change in nomenclature that has taken place—from *Negro* to *colored* to *Black* and *Afro-American,* to *Black* and *African American,* and finally to *African American* to identify all persons of African descent in the United States regardless of land of origin or time of arrival on these shores. The self-naming of Barack Obama, a young man of African and Euro-American ancestry, has played a large role in fostering this change. Now the forty-fourth president and the first African American president of the United States, Obama has consciously identified with those Africans brought to these shores in slavery; he identifies with their oppression and also with their faith.

In his autobiography, *Dreams from My Father*,[37] he identifies himself as African American rather than Black. What impact this form of naming and therefore of identity will have on the African American community at large, both religious and secular, is yet to be seen, but it is hoped it will serve as a point of unity rather than one of ongoing dissension.

The Faith Journey Continues

In 1984 the Black Catholic bishops of the United States declared that there comes a time when people come to their maturity and proclaim the faith that is theirs. African American Christians are fully mature in their faith today; indeed, the variations in how they articulate that faith in the Divine, someone greater than themselves, continue to grow and multiply. Throughout this work I have tried to show that African American (Black) spirituality is as varied as those who have helped to develop it. It is not possible to say that there is only one form of that spirituality because every generation has made its own contribution to that "river of spirituality" that flows from Africa to and through the United States and is now becoming a critical aspect of the African Diaspora. As some traditions and forms of ritual become less common, others appear that are seemingly new but have their roots nonetheless in those traditions flowing back to Africa.

As we see a return to indigenous African religious traditions, especially Yoruban beliefs and practices, brought by the many new immigrants from Africa to the United States, we also see a renewed desire to connect with and bring forth the history and traditions of the religion of the slaves. We seek *sankofa*, a return to the past to excavate and retrieve that which is good in order to move forward into the future, a future still fraught with dangers and obstacles for persons of African ancestry.

The battle is not yet over. Although the election of the first African American president has brought about many changes, it has also sadly triggered a negative reaction, especially by those who apparently still cannot accept that Black Americans are permanently present in the United States and are growing in educational, intellectual, and other skills. They have begun to take their places in helping to build up this country into the true land of freedom and equality for all.

At the same time, we find ourselves confronted by our young adults, male and female. As Patricia Hill Collins notes, the generation that grew up in the aftermath of the civil rights and Black Power movements experienced a "period of initial promise, profound change, and, for far too many, heart-wrenching disappointment." It was this generation that "lived the shift from a color-conscious racism that relied on strict racial segregation to a seemingly colorblind racism that promised equal opportunities yet provided no lasting avenues for African American advancement." This new colorblind racism has managed to "replicate racial hierarchy as effectively as the racial segregation of old."[38]

The members of this generation and of those coming after it find themselves restricted and hemmed in by a racism far more insidious in many ways because it is hidden. Their response to this situation can be found expressed, as in generations before, in music, dance, sermons, and prayer. They are represented by new forms of preachers as well as by the emergence of a new generation of Black ministers, many of whom are women, who continue to challenge the reality that confronts them. Through gospel, hip-hop, and rap music, and the emergence of nondenominational mega-churches, they are helping to develop yet another phase of Black spirituality that continues to be a spirituality of resistance.

The Black presence is a subversive presence in the United States because it calls forth a subversive memory, one that subverts reality by exposing the often sordid truths behind the claims we make about ourselves as a nation and a people. Our very existence invokes the memory of the horrors of slavery and Jim Crow and forces acknowledgment of the reality that the social constructs of racism, sexism, and ethnocentrism were not overcome but still persist. Yet, we as a people still have hope in and continue to work for what can still yet be, a nation of equals where all men and women are free to live their lives as they so desire.

African American spirituality persists. It grounds African Americans in their past but helps to free them for their future. It is a potent source of energy released through the Holy Spirit that feeds their souls and sustains them over rough places and smooth. It is found in the moaning cry of a mother who finds herself without a job or a home and with children to feed but who fights to keep her family together. It is heard in the angry voices of those who protest the closing of schools in Black neighborhoods and the denial of decent education to so many who are poor. It is to be seen in the efforts of so many Black teachers who buy needed supplies for their children because the children's parents cannot afford to buy them. It is heard in the growing number of women's voices who are preaching the gospel despite the obstacles and resistance to their ministries. African American spirituality is found still in the wail of the jazz saxophone and the pounding of the gospel piano, in the rap and hip-hop songs of today's Black youth as they protest against the conditions in which they live. Black/African American spirituality enables Black Americans to keep their "eyes on the prize and hold on," knowing that God is still with them and continues to guide them enabling them to move upward and onward toward the "kin-dom."[39]

Notes

Introduction

1. Lawrence W. Levine, *Black Culture, Black Consciousness: Afro-American Folk Thought from Slavery to Freedom* (New York: Oxford University Press, 1977), xi.

2. The definition of who is African American and who is Black American still receives heated discussion and debate in the Black community. Today most media outlets conflate the two terms and use them interchangeably. I will be doing the same throughout this text. But it is important to note that historically African American was seen as a subset of Black Americans. The term *African American* applied to those persons of African descent born in the United States whose ancestry dated back to the period of slavery, whether their ancestors were actually slaves or free persons. Black Americans, the umbrella term, applied to all persons of African descent living in the United States regardless of place of birth of themselves or their ancestors. This includes Caribbean Americans, Nigerian Americans, and so forth. The election of Barack Obama as the first Black president of the United States has, in part, caused the increased blurring. Under the historical definition, he would be seen as Black rather than African American. His example, however, is breaking down many of the barriers and resistance that have unfortunately existed in the Black community in the United States between those of African descent from different nations and those indigenous, after more than four hundred years of residency, to this country.

3. "Seasoning" denotes the practice of bringing new imports of Africans to one of the Caribbean islands where they were literally trained to be slaves, to accept their situation, and to learn passivity and obedience. It was also called "breaking in." The seasoning was very harsh, enforced with whips, chains, and other destructive means against any who fought against their enslavement. Often it led to the death of individual slaves. Over time, the colonies (the fledgling states) began to do their own seasoning of both imported and U.S.-born slaves who continued to resist their enslavement. For more, see Frederick Douglass, "The Negro Breaker," in *The Life and*

Times of Frederick Douglass (Mineola, NY: Dover Books, 2003), 140–54.

4. The Middle Passage (also today referred to as *Maafa* and the African Holocaust) was the middle leg of the African slave trade that started usually in England, then went to the coast of West Africa, where Africans were forcibly imprisoned on ships and taken to different parts of the Americas. The last leg of the trip was back to England. *Maafa* is Swahili for "disaster, terrible occurrence or great tragedy," marking the horrors of the journey that took place where countless Africans died of disease, injuries, and starvation over the typically fifty-day journey. See Marcus Rediker, *The Slave Ship: A Human History* (New York: Penguin, 2008); and Hugh Thomas, *The Slave Trade: The Story of the Atlantic Slave Trade 1440–1870* (New York: Simon and Schuster, 1999). It is believed that in the almost five hundred years of the *Maafa* approximately ten million Africans were brought to the United States. This number does not, however, reflect the actual numbers taken from Africa. Estimates range from forty million to one hundred million, of which the great majority died or were killed.

5. Levine, *Black Culture, Black Consciousness.*

6. See Black Bishops of the United States, "Our Spirituality and Its Gifts," in *What We Have Seen and Heard* (Cincinnati: St. Anthony Messenger Press, 1984), 8–11.

1. What Is Africa to Me?

1. Countee Cullen, "What Is Africa to Me?" in *The Poetry of Black America*, ed. Gwendelyn Brooks and Arnold Adoff (New York: Harper and Row, 1973), 88–91. Copyrights held by Amistad Research Center, Tulane University. Administered by Thompson and Thompson, Brooklyn, NY.

2. Many of the first Africans were brought to the Americas by the Portuguese, Spanish, and French explorers of the Southwest and Southeast. Many were free men and women, not slaves, who colonized and intermarried with both Europeans and Indians. See Cyprian Davis, *The History of Black Catholics in the United States* (New York: Crossroad, 1990).

3. Cullen, "What Is Africa to Me?," 90.

4. Ibid., 90.

5. Jamie T. Phelps, OP, "Inculturating Jesus: A Search for Dynamic Images for the Mission of the Church among African

Americans," in *Taking Down Our Harps: Black Catholics in the United States*, ed. Diana L. Hayes and Cyprian Davis, OSB (Maryknoll, NY: Orbis Books, 1999), 179–80.

6. Agbonkhianmeghe E. Orobator, *Theology Brewed in an African Pot* (Maryknoll, NY: Orbis Books, 2008), 141.

7. Benjamin C. Ray, *African Religions: Symbol, Ritual, and Community*, 2nd ed. (New York: Prentice Hall, 1999), xii.

8. Ibid.

9. Maulana Karenga, "Black Religion: The African Model," in *Down by the Riverside: Readings in African American Religion*, ed. Larry Murphy (New York: New York University Press, 2000), 42.

10. Albert Raboteau, *Slave Religion: The "Invisible Institution" in the Antebellum South* (New York: Oxford University Press, 1978), 16.

11. Jacob Olupona, *African Spirituality: Forms, Meanings and Expressions* (New York: Crossroad, 2001), xv.

12. Ray, *African Religions*, 45.

13. Joseph O. Awolalu, "The Encounter between African Traditional Religion and Other Religions in Nigeria," in *African Traditional Religion in Contemporary Society*, ed. Jacob Olupona (St. Paul: Paragon House, 1991), 111.

14. Orobator, *Theology Brewed in an African Pot*, 21.

15. Ibid., 20.

16. Ibid., 21.

17. Vincent Mulago, "Traditional African Religions and Christianity," in Olupona, *African Traditional Religion in Contemporary Society*, 119.

18. Karenga, "Black Religion," 42.

19. Ibid., 43.

20. Ibid.

21. Ibid.

22. As discussed in John Mbiti, *African Religions and Philosophy* (Garden City, NY: Doubleday Anchor, 1970), 1–7.

23. Karenga, "Black Religion," 43.

24. Ibid.

25. Ibid., 44.

26. Mulago, "Traditional African Religions and Christianity," 120.

27. Ibid., 121.

28. Ibid., 122.

29. Ibid.

30. Orobator, *Theology Brewed in an African Pot*, 62.

31. Ibid.

32. Ibid., 125–26.

33. Ibid.

34. Ibid., 127.

35. Ibid., 140–41.

36. Olupona, *African Spirituality*, xvii.

37. Dominique Zahan, *The Religion, Spirituality, and Thought of Traditional Africa* (Chicago: University of Chicago Press, 1983), xvi.

38. Ray, *African Religions*, 1.

39. Orobator, *Theology Brewed in an African Pot*, 44.

40. Ibid., 45.

41. Ibid., 48.

42. Olupona, *African Spirituality*, xvi.

43. Robert B. Fisher, *West African Religious Traditions: Focus on the Akan of Ghana* (Maryknoll, NY: Orbis Books, 1998), 19.

44. Ibid., 15.

45. Ibid., 16.

46. Ibid.

47. Ray, *African Religions*, 48.

48. Ibid., 49.

49. Ibid., 59.

50. Fisher, *West African Religious Traditions*, 16.

51. Ibid., 17.

52. Olupona, *African Spirituality*, xvi.

53. Ibid., xxii.

54. Orobator, *Theology Brewed in an African Pot*, 75–76.

55. Ibid., 146.

56. Dominque Zahan, "Some Perspectives on African Spirituality," cited in Olupona, *African Spirituality*, 3.

2. "Lord, How Come Me Here?"

1. Peter J. Paris, *The Spirituality of African Peoples* (Minneapolis: Fortress Press, 1994), 22.

2. Distinctions in skin color did not become a critical issue until Africans began to be imported into the Americas for enslavement. An excellent brief discussion of the development of "whiteness"

in distinction to "blackness" can be found in Anna Stubblefield, "History in Black: The Construction of Black Identity and White Supremacy," in *Ethics along the Color Line* (Ithaca, NY: Cornell University Press, 2005), 21–69.

3. *Dred Scott v. Sanford* (1857).

4. Among the most successful was the Amistad Rebellion, which resulted in a trial in Boston that led to the freeing of the captives who had been bound for enslavement in Cuba. The television miniseries *Roots* (1977) shows clearly in Parts 1 and 2 how a shipboard rebellion was planned and those enslaved below decks were able to overcome language and other issues to unite as one people in defense of their lives.

5. *Sankofa* is an Akan word (Ghana) that means "go back and take." Since its introduction in the film of the same name in 1993, it has become a term (with accompanying symbol from the Asante Adinkra) used in the Black community to emphasize the importance of returning to one's past in order to claim one's future.

6. Kelly Brown Douglas, *What's Faith Got to do With It? Black Bodies, Christian Souls* (Maryknoll, NY: Orbis Books, 2005), 172.

7. Albert J. Raboteau, *Slave Religion: The "Invisible Institution" in the Antebellum South* (New York: Oxford University Press, 2004), 42.

8. Ibid., 48.

9. Joseph E. Holloway, ed., *Africanisms in American Culture* (Bloomington: Indiana University Press, 1990), ix.

10. Ibid., xiii.

11. Ibid.

12. Ibid., 16.

13. See William Pollitzer and David Moltke-Hansen, *The Gullah People and Their African Heritage* (Athens: University of Georgia Press, 2005). See also the work of fiction, Pat Conroy, *The Water Is Wide* (New York: Bantam Books, 1987); the film *Daughters of the Dust;* and the documentary *Family across the Sea* (1991), which reveals the many connections between the people of the Sea Islands and those of present-day Sierra Leone.

14. Pollitzer and Moltke-Hansen, *The Gullah People and Their African Heritage*, 17.

15. See Cyprian Davis, *The History of Black Catholics in the United States* (New York: Crossroad, 1990).

16. Cyprian Davis, "God of Our Weary Years: Black Catholics in American Catholic History," in *Taking Down Our Harps: Black Catholics in the United States*, ed. Diana L. Hayes and Cyprian Davis (Maryknoll, NY: Orbis Books, 1998), 20.

17. Clarence Joseph Rivers, *Spirit in Worship* (Cincinnati, OH: Stimuli, 1979), 4.

18. Jamie T. Phelps, OP, "Inculturating Jesus: A Search for Dynamic Images for the Mission of the Church among African Americans," in *Taking Down Our Harps: Black Catholics in the United States*, ed. Diana L. Hayes and Cyprian Davis (Maryknoll, NY: Orbis Books, 1998), 179.

19. John K. Thornton, "African Dimensions of the Stono Rebellion," *The American Historical Review* 96/4 (October 1991): 1103.

20. George Ofari-Atta-Thomas, "African Inheritance in Black Church Worship," *The Journal of the Interdenominational Theological Center* 14 (Fall 1986/Spring 1987): 1–2, 45.

21. See Marcus Jernegan, "Slavery and Conversion in the American Colonies," *The American Historical Review* 21 (1916): 511.

22. Charles Pinckney Jr., cited in Diana L. Hayes, *And Still We Rise: An Introduction to Black Liberation Theology* (Mahweh, NJ: Paulist Press, 1996), 33–34.

23. Charles Colcock Jones, cited in Erskine Clarke, *Wrestlin' Jacob: A Portrait of Religion in the Old South* (Louisville, KY: Westminster John Knox, 1979), 26.

24. Ibid., 27.

25. Both churches had their origins in the Church of England but eventually broke away due to their different interpretations of scripture and tradition. Both were present in the colonies but grew enormously with the impact of both Great Awakenings.

26. Raboteau, *Slave Religion*, 148.

27. See, for example, the Massachusetts Historical Society's discussion of these petitions on the www.masshist.org website.

28. Allen Dwight Callahan, *The Talking Book: African Americans and the Bible* (New Haven: Yale University Press, 2006), xii.

29. Ibid., 34.

30. Dwight Hopkins, *Shoes That Fit Our Feet: Sources for a Constructive Black Theology* (Maryknoll, NY: Orbis Books, 1993), 22.

31. Clarke, *Wrestlin' Jacob*, 40.

32. Ibid., 41.

33. Brown Douglas, *What's Faith Got to Do with It?*, 155.

34. Ibid.

35. John Lovell, *Black Song: The Forge and the Flame: The Story of How the Afro-American Spiritual Was Hammered Out* (New York: Paragon Books, 1986), 150–51.

36. Arthur Jones, *Wade in the Water: The Wisdom of the Spirituals* (Maryknoll, NY: Orbis Books, 1993), 8.

3. Say Amen, Somebody

1. Thomas Dorsey, gospel singer and composer, from documentary of same name (1982).

2. Anonymous ex-slave, in Clifton H. Johnson, ed., *God Struck Me Dead: Voices of Ex-Slaves*, new intro. Albert Raboteau (Cleveland: The Pilgrim Press, 1993), 172.

3. Calvin Bruce, "Black Spirituality, Language, and Faith," *Religious Education* 4 (July/August 1976): 63–76.

4. Flora Wilson Bridges, *Resurrection Song: African American Spirituality* (Maryknoll, NY: Orbis Books, 2001), 1–2.

5. Robert E. Hood, *Begrimed and Black: Christian Tradition on Blacks and Blackness* (Minneapolis: Fortress Press, 1994), 204.

6. See Art Rosenbaum, *Shout Because You Are Free: The African American Ring Shout Tradition in Coastal Georgia* (Athens: University of Georgia Press, 1998).

7. Albert Raboteau, *Slave Religion: The "Invisible Institution" in the Antebellum South* (New York: Oxford University Press, 1978), 72.

8. Harold Courlander, *Negro Folk Music, USA* (New York: Columbia University Press, 1963), 194–95.

9. Raboteau, *Slave Religion*, 73. The first written accounts of the shout do not appear until the 1840s, but oral witness testifies to its presence in various forms from the beginning of the importation of Africans to the Americas.

10. Ibid., 64.

11. Ibid., 65.

12. The first Black church is believed to be that of Silver Bluff, South Carolina, which was built in 1773 and later burned down by plantation owners. It is believed to be the earliest independent African American congregation. The earliest formal church institution is

the African Methodist Episcopal Church, founded in Philadelphia, Pennsylvania, in 1789.

13. Raboteau, *Slave Religion*, 62.

14. Ibid.

15. Ibid., 64.

16. Ibid.

17. In Dwight Hopkins and George Cummings, eds., *Cut Loose Your Stammering Tongue: Black Theology in the Slave Narratives* (Maryknoll, NY: Orbis Books, 1991), 35.

18. James Mellon, *Bullwhip Days: The Slaves Remember, An Oral History* (1988; reprint New York: Grove Press, 2002), 195.

19. Jean McMahon Humez, *Harriet Tubman: The Life and the Life Stories* (Madison: University of Wisconsin Press, 2003), 183.

20. See Thomas Murphy, *Jesuit Slaveholding in Maryland, 1717–1838* (New York: Routledge, 2001).

21. Ibid., 87.

22. The first acknowledged priest of African descent ordained for an American diocese was Fr. Augustus Tolton (Belleville, Illinois, 1886). There were, however, three others before him, born of an African American mother who was a slave and her owner, Michael Morris Healy, a Georgian of Irish descent. Their children were all sent to the North and passed as whites, although most people knew they were Black. Patrick Healy became the president of Georgetown University after the Civil War; his brother, Alexander Sherwood, became rector of the Boston Cathedral; and James became the second bishop of Portland, Maine.

23. Raboteau, *Slave Religion*, 148.

24. Jay P. Dolan, *Catholic Revivalism: The American Experience, 1830–1900* (Notre Dame, IN: University of Notre Dame Press, 1978), xv.

25. Diana L. Hayes, "Black Catholic Revivalism: The Emergence of a New Form of Worship," *The Journal of the Interdenominational Theological Center* 14/15 (1986–87): 102.

26. Herbert Aptheker, *American Negro Slave Revolts*, 50th anniv. ed. (New York: International Publishers, 1993), xi.

27. John Thornton, "African Dimensions of the Stono Rebellion," *The American Historical Review* 96/4 (October 1991): 1103.

28. Mark Smith, "Remembering Mary, Shaping Revolt: Reconsidering the Stono Rebellion," *The Journal of Southern History* 67/3 (August 2001): 518.

29. See Erlene Stetson, "Slavery: Some Literary and Pedagogical Considerations on the Black Female Slave," in *But Some of Us Are Brave*, ed. Gloria T. Hull, Patricia Bell Scott, and Barbara Smith (New York: Feminist Press at CUNY, 1993); and Jacqueline L. Tobin and Raymond G. Dobard, *Hidden in Plain View: A Secret Story of Quilts and the Underground Railroad* (New York: Anchor Books, 2000).

30. An excellent source for these narratives of conversion is Clifton H. Johnson, ed., *God Struck Me Dead: Voices of Ex-Slaves*, new intro. Albert Raboteau (Cleveland: The Pilgrim Press, 1993).

31. Hopkins and Cummings, *Cut Loose Your Stammering Tongue*, xvii.

4. Yet Do I Marvel

1. Countee Cullen, in *Poetry of Black America*, ed. Gwendelyn Brooks and Arnold Adoff (New York: Harper and Row, 1973), 88–89. Copyrights held by Amistad Research Center, Tulane University. Administered by Thompson and Thompson, Brooklyn, NY.

2. The slaves were forbidden literacy as it was feared by their owners that this would make them dissatisfied with their situation.

3. Samuel A. Floyd, Jr., *The Power of Black Music: Interpreting Its History from Africa to the United States* (New York: Oxford University Press, 1995), 39.

4. Albert J. Raboteau, *Slave Religion: The "Invisible Institution" in the Antebellum South* (New York: Oxford University Press, 1978), 23.

5. Floyd, *The Power of Black Music*, 39.

6. W. E. B. Du Bois, *The Souls of Black Folk*, new intro. Randall Kenan (New York: Penguin Group/Signet Classics, 1995), 274.

7. Ibid., 52.

8. Ibid., 265.

9. Ibid., 269–70.

10. Floyd, *The Power of Black Music*, 39.

11. Benjamin E. Mays, *The Negro's God as Reflected in His Literature* (Boston: Chapman and Grines, 1938), vii.

12. Benjamin E. Mays, *The Negro's Church* (New York: Institute of Social and Religious Research, 1933).

13. Mays, *The Negro's God as Reflected in His Literature*, 14.

14. Ibid., 21.

15. Ibid., 23–24.

16. Gayraud S. Wilmore, *Black Religion and Black Radicalism: An Interpretation of the Religious History of Afro-American People*, 2nd ed., rev. (Maryknoll, NY: Orbis Books, 1983), 225.

17. James H. Cone, *The Spirituals and the Blues* (1972; reprint, Maryknoll, NY: Orbis Books, 1992), 4.

18. Ibid., 4.

19. Ibid., 4, 5, 6.

20. Floyd, *The Power of Black Music*, 40.

21. John Lovell, "The Social Implications of the Negro Spiritual," in *The Social Implications of Early Negro Music in the United States*, ed. Bernard Katz (New York: Arno Press, 1969), 136, as cited in Cone, *The Spirituals and the Blues*, 13 (see note 19); see also John Lovell, *Black Song: The Forge and the Flame: The Story of How the African American Spiritual Was Hammered Out* (New York: Paragon House, 1986).

22. Lovell, "The Social Implications of the Negro Spiritual," 132, as cited in Cone, *The Spirituals and the Blues*, 14.

23. Ibid., 134–35, 14.

24. Cone, *The Spirituals and the Blues*, 27.

25. Ibid., 29.

26. Ibid., 32.

27. Du Bois, *Souls of Black Folk*, 275–76.

28. James Weldon Johnson and J. Rosamund Johnson, *The Book of American Negro Spirituals* (New York: Da Capo Press, 1977), 49.

29. See Douglas Blackmon, *Slavery by Another Name: The Re-enslavement of Black Americans from The Civil War to World War II* (New York: Doubleday, 2008).

30. Floyd, *The Power of Black Music*, 41.

5. Oh, Freedom!

1. Albert Raboteau, *Slave Religion: The "Invisible Institution" in the Antebellum South* (New York: Oxford University Press, 1978), 136–37.

2. Gayraud S. Wilmore, *Black Religion and Black Radicalism: An Interpretation of the Religious History of Afro-American People*, 2nd ed., rev. (Maryknoll, NY: Orbis Books, 1983), 76.

3. Ibid., 77.

4. D. A. Cook and C. Y. Wiley, "Psychotherapy with Members of African American Churches and Spiritual Traditions," in *Handbook of Psychotherapy and Religious Diversity*, ed. P. S. Richards and A. E. Bergin (Washington DC: American Psychology Association, 2000), 369.

5. Barbara A. Holmes, *Unspeakable Joy: Contemplative Practices of the Black Church* (Minneapolis: Fortress Press, 2004), 4.

6. M. Shawn Copeland, "Foundations for Catholic Theology in an African American Context," in *Black and Catholic: The Challenge and Gift of Black Faith*, ed. Jamie T. Phelps (Milwaukee: Marquette University Press, 1997), 140.

7. Mumia Abu-Jamal, *Faith of Our Fathers: An Examination of the Spiritual Life of African and African American People* (New York: Africa World Press, 2003), 98.

8. Leonard Gadzekpo, "The Black Church, Slavery, the Civil Rights Movement and the Future," *The Journal of Religious Thought* 53/54, nos. 2/1 (1997): 98.

9. Ibid.

10. Wilmore, *Black Religion and Black Radicalism*, 95.

11. Raboteau, *Slave Religion*, 209.

12. Ibid., 137.

13. Stacey Floyd-Thomas et al., eds. *Black Church Studies: An Introduction* (Nashville, TN: Abingdon Press, 2007), xxiii.

14. W. E. B. Du Bois, "The Problem of Amusement," in *W. E. B. Du Bois: On Sociology and the Black Community*, ed. Dan Green and Edward Driver (Chicago: University of Chicago Press, 1978), 226, as cited in Curtis J. Evans, *The Burden of Black Religion* (New York: Oxford University Press, 2008), 152.

15. W. E. B. Du Bois, *The Negro Church* (1903) (reprint with intro. Phil Zuckerman et al. [Walnut Creek: Alta Mira Press, 2003]), i, as cited in Evans, *The Burden of Black Religion*, 156. In Du Bois's time those actively working on issues concerning the Black community were called race men and race women. As persons of faith, their actions affected the Black church and its life of worship. A Black or race life of worship was measured in numbers of congregations or race units.

16. Black Catholic Bishops of the United States, "What We Have Seen and Heard" (Cincinnati: St. Anthony Messenger Press, 1984), 15.

17. W. E. B. Du Bois, "The Gift of the Spirit," in *W. E. B. Du Bois: A Reader*, ed. David Levering Lewis (New York: Henry Holt, 1995), 57.

18. Cook and Wiley, "Psychotherapy with Members of African American Churches and Spiritual Traditions," 370.

19. The first African American priest, Augustus Tolton, was ordained in Rome in 1886. Most American bishops refused to ordain Black men until the twentieth century; an exception was the Society of St. Joseph, which ordained Charles Uncles in 1891.

20. The earlier dates apply to when Black Methodists left the white church of which they had been less than full members and began to work toward developing new religious institutions of their own. The later date is when the particular church institution was formalized under Black leadership.

21. Wilmore, *Black Religion and Black Radicalism*, 82

22. Ibid., 82–83.

23. Ira Berlin, *The Making of African America: The Four Great Migrations* (New York: Viking Adult, 2010), 147.

24. Wilmore, *Black Religion and Black Radicalism*, 78.

25. Floyd-Thomas et al., *Black Church Studies*, 23.

26. Delores Williams, *Sisters in the Wilderness: Womanist Theology* (Maryknoll, NY: Orbis Books, 1995), 204–5.

27. Ibid., 206.

28. Holmes, *Unspeakable Joy*, 5.

29. See Douglas Blackmon, *Slavery by Another Name: The Re-enslavement of Black Americans from the Civil War to World War II* (New York: Doubleday, 2008).

30. Jim Crow was a system of *de jure* segregation established in the Southern (and some few other) states in the United States between 1876 (the end of Reconstruction) and 1965 (the passage of the Civil Rights Act of 1964). It covered all aspects of public and private life and mandated strict segregation between Blacks and whites.

31. Nell Irvin Painter, *Creating Black America: African American History and Its Meanings, 1619 to the Present* (New York: Oxford University Press, 2006), 130.

32. Ibid., 129.

33. Ibid., 135.

34. See Emmett Curran, "'Splendid Poverty': Jesuit Slaveholding in Maryland, 1805–1838," in *Catholics in the Old South: Essays*

on *Church and Culture*, ed. Randall Miller (Macon, GA: Mercer University Press, 1999), 125–47.

35. W. E. B. Du Bois, "The Crisis (July 1915)," as cited in Wilmore, *Black Religion and Black Radicalism*, 138.

36. Wilmore, *Black Religion and Black Radicalism*, 139.

37. Ibid., 140.

38. Ibid., 136.

39. Ibid., 224.

40. See James H. Cone's fuller discussion in *The Spirituals and the Blues* (1972; reprint, Maryknoll, NY: Orbis Books, 1992).

41. Wilmore, *Black Religion and Black Radicalism*, 225.

42. Du Bois, *The Souls of Black Folk*, with a new introduction by Randall Kenan (New York: Penguin Group/Signet Classics, 1995), 225.

43. E. U. Essien-Udom, as discussed in Wilmore, *Black Religion and Black Radicalism*, 133–34.

6. My Soul Is Rested

1. Mrs. Pollard was responding to those who suggested she not participate any further in the Montgomery Bus Boycott because of her age, as cited in Taylor Branch, *Parting the Waters: America in the King Years 1954–1963* (New York: Simon and Schuster, 1988), 149.

2. Song composed and sung by Sam Cooke, 1964.

3. For an in-depth discussion of the Great Migration, see Isabel Wilkerson, *The Warmth of Other Suns: The Epic Story of America's Great Migration* (New York: Random House, 2010).

4. Ibid.

5. See Douglas L. Blackmon, *Slavery by Another Name: The Re-enslavement of Black Americans from the Civil War to World War II* (New York: Doubleday, 2009).

6. Gayraud S. Wilmore, *Black Religion and Black Radicalism: An Interpretation of the Religious History of African Americans*, 2nd ed., rev. (1973; reprint, Maryknoll, NY: Orbis Books, 1983), 225.

7. Ibid., 224.

8. See James H. Cone, *The Spirituals and the Blues* (1972; reprint, Maryknoll, NY: Orbis Books, 1992).

9. See "Beginnings," in Isabel Wilkerson, *The Warmth of Other Suns: The Epic Story of America's Great Migration* (New York: Random House, 2010). Pastors who supported their congregants' flights toward freedom often found themselves arrested by city and state officials enforcing hastily passed laws forbidding the "encouragement" of Black migration.

10. Race riots and lynchings increased every time a Black soldier or sailor came home in uniform.

11. "Strange Fruit" is a song made famous by Billie Holiday, based on a poem by Abel Meeropol. The strange fruit was the dangling tortured bodies of Blacks killed for stepping out of their "rightful place."

12. Randolph headed the Brotherhood of Sleeping Car Porters, the largest Black union in its time, and was a key leader in the Civil Rights movement.

13. A phrase made popular in the aftermath of the Second Vatican Council (1963–65) in Rome as a basis for the Catholic and other churches becoming more involved on the social, economic, and political levels of modern society.

14. Martin Luther King Jr., "Where Do We Go from Here?," speech to the Southern Christian Leadership Conference in Atlanta, Georgia, August 16, 1967. Available online.

15. Howard Thurman, *Jesus and the Disinherited* (Nashville, TN: Abingdon Press, 1949), 13.

16. See James Evans, *We Have Been Believers: An African American Systematic Theology* (Minneapolis: Fortress Press, 1992), 83–84.

17. Howard Thurman, *Footprints of a Dream* (Eugene, OR: Wipf and Stock, 2009), 27.

18. See Taylor Branch, "Forerunner: Vernon Johns," *Parting the Waters: America in the King Years 1954–1963* (New York: Simon and Schuster, 1989), 1–27.

19. Quoted in Patrick L. Cooney and Henry W. Powell, *The Life and Times of the Prophet Vernon Johns: Father of the Civil Rights Movement* (1998), chap. 2. Available online at www.vernonjohns.org/tcal001.propht.html.

20. Martin Luther King Jr., "Nobel Peace Prize Acceptance Speech" (1964).

21. Martin Luther King Jr., "Letter from a Birmingham Jail" (1963).

22. James Cleveland, gospel song, "Please Be Patient with Me, God Is Not Through with Me Yet."

23. See Vanessa White, "Somebody's Callin' My Name: Discerning Worship in the African American Community," paper written in fulfillment of Doctor of Ministry requirements, Catholic Theological Union, Chicago, 2005.

24. Coretta Scott King, "Foreword," *Standing in the Need of Prayer* (New York: The Free Press, 2003), x. Available online.

25. Jamie T. Phelps, "Black Spirituality," in *Spiritual Traditions for the Contemporary Church*, ed. Robin Maas and Gabriel O'Donnell (Nashville, TN: Abingdon Press, 1990), 344–45.

26. This protest song became the theme song, as it were, for the Civil Rights movement. It is based on a gospel song by Charles Albert Tindley, but the lyrics were frequently changed to fit the situation taking place during the movement.

27. "Black Power: A Statement by the National Committee of Negro Churchmen" (July 1, 1966), in *Black Theology: A Documentary History, Vol. 1, 1966–1979*, ed. James H. Cone and Gayraud S. Wilmore (Maryknoll, NY: Orbis Books, 1993), 19.

28. King, "Where Do We Go from Here?"

29. Turner became a proponent of the Return to Africa Movement of the late 1800s. Garvey, founder of the Universal Negro Improvement Association, promoted a return to Africa for persons of African descent in his Africa for the Africans effort.

30. After a pilgrimage to Mecca (the Hajj) where he encountered Muslims of all races and ethnicities, Malcolm X repudiated the racist teachings of the Nation.

31. See Diana L. Hayes, *And Still We Rise: An Introduction to Black Liberation Theology* (Mahwah, NJ: Paulist Press, 1996), 68.

32. "Black Theology," statement of the National Committee of Black Churchmen (1969), in Cone and Wilmore, *Black Theology*, 38.

33. They would later come to recognize that not just race but gender and class were also critical factors in the ongoing oppression of African Americans.

34. See James H. Cone, *Black Theology and Black Power* (1969; reprint, Maryknoll, NY: Orbis Books, 1997); and idem, *A Black Theology of Liberation* (1970; reprint, Maryknoll, NY: Orbis Books, 2010).

35. James H. Cone, *God of the Oppressed* (1975; reprint, Maryknoll, NY: Orbis Books, 1997), 136.

36. Evans, *We Have Been Believers*, 91–92.

37. Albert Cleage, *The Black Messiah* (Kansas City: Sheed and Ward, 1968), 111.

38. Carlyle Stewart Fielding, *Soul Survivors: An African American Spirituality* (Louisville, KY: Westminster John Knox, 1977), 23.

39. Darlene Clark Hine, *Black Women in America*, 2nd ed. (New York: Oxford University Press, 2005), 852.

40. The National Black Catholic Congress has its roots in a series of Catholic lay-led congresses that were held between 1880 and 1900 in the United States as a means for lay Black Catholics to discuss and prioritize the issues and concerns they had with the Roman Catholic Church. The contemporary congress was initiated in 1987 in Washington DC, where Black Catholics (lay, religious, and clergy) met to develop a pastoral plan for Black Catholics. The congress meets every five years.

41. National Black Catholic Clergy Caucus, "A Statement of the Black Catholic Clergy Caucus, 1968," in *Stamped with the Image of God: African Americans as God's Image in Black*, ed. Cyprian Davis and Jamie T. Phelps (Maryknoll, NY: Orbis Books, 2003), 111–13.

42. Jamie T. Phelps, "African American Catholics: The Struggles, Contributions and Gifts of a Marginalized Community," in *Black and Catholic: The Challenge and Gift of Black Folk* (Milwaukee: Marquette University Press, 1997), 21, 18.

43. Hayes, *And Still We Rise*, 171–72.

44. Wilmore, *Black Religion and Black Radicalism*, 191.

7. Beautiful Are the Souls of My Black Sisters

1. Parts of this chapter were previously published in "Faith of Our Mothers: Catholic Womanist God-Talk," in *Uncommon Faithfulness: The Black Catholic Experience*, ed. M. Shawn Copeland (Maryknoll, NY: Orbis Books, 2009), 128–46.

2. "My People," in *The Collected Poems of Langston Hughes*, ed. Arnold Rampersad (New York: Vintage, 1995), 36.

3. Historically, Black feminists emerged from the larger feminist movement that was predominantly white and organized around issues of gender; womanism began as a theological movement of African American Christian women and addressed issues of race, class, gender, and sexuality.

4. See Delores S. Williams, *Sisters in the Wilderness: The Challenge of Womanist God-Talk* (Maryknoll, NY: Orbis Books, 1995).

5. Some women attempted to remain celibate and others refused to bring a child into the world of slavery using herbs and other means of abortion, while others committed infanticide in preference to seeing their child raised as a slave. See Darlene Clark Hine, "Female Slave Resistance: The Economics of Sex," in *Black Women in America*, vol. 2 (Brooklyn: Carlson, 1992), 657–66.

6. Meaning that they were made perfect in the eyes of God because of their harsh situations despite the fact that they were seen as less than perfect and even less than human in the eyes of white Americans.

7. Bernice Johnson Reagon, "African Diaspora Women: The Making of Cultural Workers," in *Women in Africa and the African Diaspora*, ed. Rosalyn Terborg-Penn et al. (Washington DC: Howard University Press, 1987), 169.

8. Laverne McCain Gill, *Daughters of Dignity: African Women in the Bible and the Virtues of Black Womanhood* (Cleveland: Pilgrim Press, 2000), xiv–xv.

9. Bettye Collier-Thomas, *Jesus, Jobs, and Justice: African American Women and Religion* (New York: Knopf, 2010), 169.

10. As we shall see herein, African American women still seek out those women in the Bible who speak to their present-day situation. In doing so, they have discovered and recovered new/old voices: Eve, Mary Magdalene, and Mary the Mother of God as models to emulate.

11. Civilla Martin and Charles Gabriel, "His Eye Is on the Sparrow," gospel song (1905).

12. Alice Walker, *In Search of Our Mothers' Gardens: Womanist Prose* (New York: Harcourt Brace Jovanovich, 1983), 231.

13. As previously discussed, the African Methodist Episcopal Church began by the departure of Black members from St. George's Methodist Church because of the negative treatment they received from white congregants. What is not as well known is that Black Catholics also often walked out of white churches and petitioned for their own freestanding churches because of the discriminatory treatment they received. Although the priests were still white in these Black parishes, the parishioners had greater control over activities, liturgy, and other aspects of parish and worship life. See, for example, Morris Macgregor, *The Emergence of a Black*

Catholic Community: St. Augustine's in Washington (Washington DC: Catholic University of America Press, 1999).

14. See Flora Wilson Bridges, *Resurrection Song: African American Spirituality* (Maryknoll, NY: Obis Books, 2001), 43–82.

15. Ibid., 92–93.

16. Williams, *Sisters in the Wilderness*, 39.

17. Ibid., 39.

18. Ibid., 40.

19. Bert James Loewenberg and Ruth Bogin, *Black Women in Nineteenth-Century Life* (University Park: Pennsylvania State University Press, 1976), 167, as quoted in Williams, *Sisters in the Wilderness*, 40.

20. Williams, *Sisters in the Wilderness*, 118.

21. Ibid., 119.

22. Collier-Thomas, *Jesus, Justice, and Jobs*, xxv.

23. Walker, *In Search of Our Mothers' Gardens.*

24. Alice Walker's complete definition of womanist is:

1. From womanish. (Opp. of "girlish," i.e., frivolous, irresponsible, not serious.) A Black feminist or feminist of color. From the Black folk expression of mothers to female children, "you acting womanish," i.e., like a woman. Usually referring to outrageous, audacious, courageous or willful behavior. Wanting to know more and in greater depth than is considered "good" for one. Interested in grown up doings. Acting grown up. Being grown up. Interchangeable with another Black folk expression: "You trying to be grown." Responsible. In charge. Serious.

2. Also: A woman who loves other women, sexually and/or nonsexually. Appreciates and prefers women's culture, women's emotional flexibility (values tears as natural counterbalance of laughter), and women's strength. Sometimes loves individual men, sexually and/or nonsexually. Committed to survival and wholeness of entire people, male and female. Not a separatist, except periodically, for health. Traditionally a universalist, as in: "Mama, why are we brown, pink, and yellow, and our cousins are white, beige and black?" Ans. "Well, you know the colored race is just like a flower garden, with every color flower represented." Traditionally capable, as in: "Mama, I'm walking to Canada and I'm taking you and a bunch of other slaves with me." Reply: "It wouldn't be the first time."

3. Loves music. Loves dance. Loves the moon. Loves the Spirit. Loves love and food and roundness. Loves struggle. Loves the Folk. Loves herself. Regardless.

4. Womanist is to feminist as purple is to lavender (Walker, *In Search of Our Mothers' Gardens*, xi).

25. Diana L. Hayes, "And When We Speak: To Be Black, Catholic, and Womanist," in *Taking Down Our Harps: Black Catholics in the United States*, ed. Diana L. Hayes and Cyprian Davis, OSB (Maryknoll, NY: Orbis Books, 1999), 106.

26. Katie G. Cannon, *Black Womanist Ethics* (Atlanta, GA: Scholars Press, 1988), 8.

27. See Williams, *Sisters in the Wilderness*, 60–81, 162–67.

28. Jacquelyn Grant, "Subjectification as a Requirement for Christological Construction," in *Lift Every Voice: Constructing Theologies from the Underside*, ed. Susan Brooks Thistlethwaite and Mary Potter Engel (Maryknoll, NY: Orbis Books, 1998), 210.

29. Ibid., see 214–15.

30. Kelly Brown Douglas, *The Black Christ* (Maryknoll, NY: Orbis Books, 1994), 109–10; Jacquelyn Grant, *White Women's Christ, Black Women's Jesus* (Atlanta, GA: Scholars Press, 1989), 220.

31. JoAnne Terell, *Power in the Blood: The Cross in the African American Experience* (Maryknoll, NY: Orbis Books, 1998), 124–25.

32. Emilie Townes, *In a Blaze of Glory: Womanist Spirituality as Social Witness* (Nashville, TN: Abingdon Press, 1995), 10–11.

33. Ibid.

34. Kelly Brown Douglas, *What's Faith Got to Do with It? Black Bodies/Christian Souls* (Maryknoll, NY: Orbis Books, 2005), 155.

35. Ibid., 172.

36. Ibid., 173.

37. Bridges, *Resurrection Song*, ix.

38. Ibid., 5.

39. Ibid., 165.

40. Ibid.

41. M. Shawn Copeland, *Enfleshing Freedom: Body, Race, and Being* (Minneapolis. MN: Fortress Press, 2010).

42. Ibid., 24.

43. Audre Lorde, "Uses of the Erotic: The Erotic as Power," in *Sister Outsider: Essays and Speeches by Audre Lorde* (Trumansburg, NY: Crossing, 1985), 56, as cited in Copeland, *Enfleshing Freedom*, 64.

44. Copeland, *Enfleshing Freedom*, 64.

45. Cyprian Davis, OSB, *The History of Black Catholics in the United States* (New York: Crossroad, 1990), 32.

46. Hayes, "African American Catholic Women," in Hine, *Black Women in America*, 1:114.

47. Davis, *The History of Black Catholics in the United States*, 30.

48. Diana L. Hayes, "Ethiopia Will Stretch Forth Her Arms: The Evangelization and Education of African American Catholics," in the *Good News Bible with Deutero-Canonicals/Apocrypha: The African American Jubilee Edition* (New York: American Bible Society, 1993), 237–54.

49. Joseph A. Brown, SJ, *To Stand on the Rock: Meditations on Black Catholic Identity* (Maryknoll, NY: Orbis Books, 1998), 146.

50. Sr. Mary Bernard Deggs, *No Cross, No Crown: Black Nuns in Nineteenth-Century New Orleans* (Bloomington: Indiana University Press, 2002).

51. See Taylor Branch, *At Canaan's Edge: America in the King Years, 1963–1965* (New York: Simon and Schuster, 2006).

52. See writings by Bryan N. Massingale, Cyprian Davis, Diana L. Hayes, M. Shawn Copeland, Jamie T. Phelps, LaReine-Marie Mosely, Diane Batts Morrow, Cecilia Moore, C. Vanessa White, and many other Black Catholics who are excavating the lives and histories of their fellow Black Catholics in order to continue weaving the tapestry of African American spirituality in their midst.

53. Linda Villarose, ed., *Body and Soul: The Black Woman's Guide to Physical Health and Emotional Well-Being* (New York: HarperPerennial, 1994), 396–97.

8. We Who Believe in Freedom

1. Margaret Walker, "We Have Been Believers," in *The Poetry of Black America: Anthology of the Twentieth Century*, ed. Arnold Adoff (New York: Harper, 1973), 145.

2. See James H. Evans, Jr., *We Shall All Be Changed: Social Problems and Theological Renewal* (Minneapolis: Fortress Press, 2008), 89–108.

3. Walter Earl Fluker, "Spirituality, Ethics, and Leadership," in *Spirituality in Higher Education* 4/3 (June 2008): 1.

4. Ibid., 3.

5. See Janice Dean Willis, *Dreaming Me: Black, Baptist, and Buddhist—One Woman's Spiritual Journey* (Somerville, MA: Wisdom Publications, 2008); Angel Kyodo Williams, *Being Black: Zen and the Art of Living with Fearlessness and Grace* (New York: Penguin, 2002); Faith Adiele, *Meeting Faith: The Forest Journals of a Black Buddhist Nun* (New York: Norton, 2005).

6. Fluker, "Spirituality, Ethics, and Leadership."

7. Ibid., 3.

8. Ibid., 4.

9. Ibid.

10. Evans, *We Shall All Be Changed*, 90.

11. Peter Drucker, "The Age of Social Transformation," in Evans, *We Shall All Be Changed*, 91–92.

12. Evans, *We Shall All Be Changed*, 104.

13. Yvonne Patricia Chireau, "Hidden Traditions: Black Religion, Magic, and Alternative Spiritual Beliefs in Womanist Perspective," in *Perspectives on Womanist Theology*, ed. Jacquelyn Grant (Atlanta: ITC Press, 1995), 68.

14. Ibid., 107.

15. Peter J. Paris, *The Spirituality of African Peoples* (Minneapolis: Fortress Press, 2004).

16. Ibid., 22.

17. Ibid., 21–22, 22, 23.

18. Ibid., 25.

19. See Carlyle Fielding Stewart III, *Soul Survivors: An African American Spirituality* (Louisville, KY: Westminster John Knox, 1997); and idem, *Black Spirituality and Black Consciousness: Soul Force, Culture and Freedom in the African-American Experience* (New York: Africa World Press, 1999).

20. Stewart, *Black Spirituality and Black Consciousness*, xiii.

21. Ibid., 1.

22. Ibid., 2.

23. Ibid., 6–7.

24. Ibid., 21.

25. Ibid., 121.

26. Cornel West, interview, in Bill Moyers, *A World of Ideas, II: Public Opinions from Private Citizens* (New York: Doubleday, 1990), 105–6.

27. Ibid., 106.

28. Ibid.

29. Cornel West, *The Cornel West Reader* (New York: Basic Civitas Books, 1999), 428.

30. Gayraud S. Wilmore, *Pragmatic Spirituality: The Christian Faith through an Africentric Lens* (New York: New York University Press, 2004), 2.

31. Ibid., 3.

32. Ibid., 4.

33. Robert M. Franklin, *Another Day's Journey: Black Churches Confronting the American Crisis* (Minneapolis: Fortress Press, 1997), 41–43.

34. Bryan N. Massingale, *Racial Justice and the Catholic Church* (Maryknoll, NY: Orbis Books, 2010), 107.

35. The founder of the Nation of Islam, the Honorable Elijah Muhammad, died in 1975 and was succeeded by his son, Warith Deen Muhammad (1933–2008). In 1976, Warith Deen Muhammad disbanded the Nation of Islam, founded the American Society of Islam and, with most of the Nation's members, converted to the orthodox Sunni branch of Islam, bringing about the largest mass conversion to Islam in American history. He rejected the race-based teachings of the Nation and became an accepted part of Islam internationally. In 1981 Louis Farrakhan revived the Nation of Islam. It persists today but in significantly smaller numbers.

36. From the Negro National Anthem, "Lift Every Voice and Sing," by James Weldon Johnson and J. Rosamund Johnson.

37. Barack Obama, *Dreams from My Father: A Story of Race and Inheritance* (New York: Random House, 2004).

38. Patricia Hill Collins, *From Black Power to Hip Hop: Racism, Nationalism, and Feminism* (Philadelphia: Temple University Press, 2006), 3.

39. I deliberately use *kin-dom* rather than *kingdom* to express the belief that God's promise is not just for a far-off heaven but for a new life here on earth where we recognize our kinship as brothers and sisters created by the same loving God and called into God's service to love one another, and where we work to bring about God's beloved community.

Selected Bibliography

African Traditional Religions/Spirituality

Fisher, Robert. *West African Religious Traditions: Focus on the Akan of Ghana*. Maryknoll, NY: Orbis Books, 1998.

Karenga, Maulana. "Black Religion: The African Model." In *Down by the Riverside: Readings in African American Religion*, edited by Larry Murphy. New York: New York University Press, 2000.

Magesa, Laurenti. *African Religion: The Moral Traditions of Abundant Life*. Maryknoll, NY: Orbis Books, 1997.

Mbiti, John. *African Religions and Philosophy*. Garden City, NY: Doubleday Anchor, 1970.

Olupona, Jacob. *African Spirituality: Forms, Meanings, and Expressions*. New York: Crossroad, 2001.

———, ed. *African Traditional Religion in Contemporary Society*. New York: New Era Books, 1991.

Orobator, Agbonkhianmeghe E. *Theology Brewed in an African Pot*. Maryknoll, NY: Orbis Books, 2008.

Ray, Benjamin C. *African Religions: Symbol, Ritual, and Community*, 2nd edition. New York: Prentice Hall, 1999.

Zahan, Dominique. *The Religion, Spirituality, and Thought of Traditional Africa*. Chicago: University of Chicago Press, 1983.

African American Culture: Slavery to the Present Day

Adoff, Arnold. *The Poetry of Black America*. New York: Harper and Row, 1973.

Aptheker, Herbert. *American Negro Slave Revolts*. 50th anniversary edition. New York: International Publishers, 1993 (1943).

Berlin, Ira. *The Making of African America: The Four Great Migrations*. New York: Viking Adult, 2010.

Blackmon, Douglas. *Slavery by Another Name: The Re-enslavement of Black Americans from the Civil War to World War II*. New York: Doubleday, 2008.

Clarke, Erskine. *Wrestlin' Jacob: A Portrait of Religion in the Old South.* Louisville, KY: Westminster John Knox, 1979.

Collier-Thomas, Bettye. *Jesus, Jobs, and Justice: African American Women and Religion.* New York: Knopf, 2010.

Collins, Patricia Hill. *From Black Power to Hip Hop: Racism, Nationalism, and Feminism.* Philadelphia: Temple University Press, 2006.

Courlander, Harold. *Negro Folk Music, USA.* New York: Columbia University Press, 1963.

Du Bois, W. E. B. *The Souls of Black Folk.* New introduction by Randall Kenan. New York: Penguin Group/Signet Classics, 1995.

Evans, Jr., Curtis H. *The Burden of Black Religion.* New York: Oxford University Press, 2008.

Floyd, Jr., Samuel A. *The Power of Black Music: Interpreting Its History from Africa to the United States.* New York: Oxford University Press, 1995.

Floyd-Thomas, Stacey, et al., eds. *Black Church Studies: An Introduction.* Nashville, TN: Abingdon Press, 2007.

Franklin, Robert M. *Another Day's Journey: Black Churches Confronting the American Crisis.* Minneapolis: Fortress Press, 1997.

Holloway, Joseph, ed. *Africanisms in American Culture.* Bloomington: Indiana University Press, 1990.

Holmes, Barbara A. *Unspeakable Joy: Contemplative Practices of the Black Church.* Minneapolis: Fortress Press, 2004.

Hood, Robert E. *Begrimed and Black: Christian Tradition on Blacks and Blackness.* Minneapolis: Fortress Press, 1994.

Hopkins, Dwight. *Shoes That Fit Our Feet.* Maryknoll, NY: Orbis Books, 1993.

Hopkins, Dwight, and George Cummings, eds. *Cut Loose Your Stammering Tongue: Black Theology in the Slave Narratives.* Maryknoll, NY: Orbis Books, 1991.

Johnson, Clifton H., ed. *God Struck Me Dead: Voices of Ex-Slaves.* New introduction by Albert Raboteau. Cleveland: The Pilgrim Press, 1993.

Johnson, James Weldon, and J. Rosamund Johnson. *The Book of American Negro Spirituals.* Two volumes in one. New York: Da Capo Press, 1977.

Jones, Arthur. *Wade in the Water: The Wisdom of the Spirituals*. Maryknoll, NY: Orbis Books, 1993.

Lovell, John. *Black Song: The Forge and the Flame: The Story of How the Afro-American Spiritual Was Hammered Out*. New York: Paragon House, 1986.

Mays, Benjamin. *The Negro's Church*. New York: Institute of Social and Religious Research, 1933.

———. *The Negro's God as Reflected in His Literature*. Boston: Chapman and Grines, 1938.

Mellon, James. *Bullwhip Days: The Slaves Remember: An Oral History*. New York: Grove Press, 2002.

Obama, Barack. *Dreams from My Father: A Story of Race and Inheritance*. New York: Random House, 2004.

Painter, Nell. *Creating Black America: African American History and Its Meanings, 1619 to the Present*. New York: Oxford University Press, 2006.

Pollitzer, William, and David Moltke-Hansen. *The Gullah People and Their African Heritage*. Athens: University of Georgia Press, 2005.

Raboteau, Albert. *Slave Religion: The "Invisible Institution" in the Antebellum South*. New York: Oxford University Press, 1978.

Rediker, Marcus. *The Slave Ship: A Human History*. New York: Penguin, 2008.

Rosenbaum, Art. *Shout Because You Are Free: The African American Ring Shout Tradition in Coastal Georgia*. Athens: University of Georgia Press, 1998.

Stubblefield, Anna. *Ethics along the Color Line*. Ithaca, NY: Cornell University Press, 2005.

Terborg-Penn, Rosalyn, et al., eds. *Women in Africa and the African Diaspora*. Washington DC: Howard University Press, 1987.

Thomas, Hugh. *The Slave Trade: The Story of the Atlantic Slave Trade 1440–1870*. New York: Simon and Schuster, 1999.

Tobin, Jacqueline. *Hidden in Plain View: A Secret Story of Quilts and the Underground Railroad*. New York: Anchor Books, 2000.

Wilkerson, Isabel. *The Warmth of Other Suns: The Epic Story of America's Great Migration*. New York: Random House, 2010.

African American Spirituality

Abu-Jamal, Mumia. *Faith of Our Fathers: An Examination of the Spiritual Life of African and African American People.* New York: Africa World Press, 2003.

Bridges, Flora Wilson. *Resurrection Song: African American Spirituality.* Maryknoll, NY: Orbis Books, 2001.

Fielding, Carlyle Stewart III. *Black Spirituality and Black Consciousness: Soul Force, Culture and Freedom in the African-American Experience.* New York: Africa World Press, 1999.

———. *Soul Survivors: An African American Spirituality.* Louisville, KY: Westminster John Knox, 1977.

Hayes, Diana L. *Trouble Don't Last Always: Soul Prayers.* Collegeville, MN: Liturgical Press, 1995.

Paris, Peter J. *The Spirituality of African Peoples.* Minneapolis: Fortress Press, 1994.

Thurman, Howard. *Jesus and the Disinherited.* Nashville, TN: Abingdon Press, 1949.

Wilmore, Gayraud S. *Pragmatic Spirituality: The Christian Faith through an Africentric Lens.* New York: New York University Press, 2004.

African Americans and the Bible

Blount, Brian, ed. *True to Our Native Land: An African American New Testament Commentary.* Minneapolis: Fortress Press, 2007.

Callahan, Allen Dwight. *The Talking Book: African Americans and the Bible.* New Haven, CT: Yale University Press, 2006.

Gill, Laverne McCain. *Daughters of Dignity: African Women in the Bible and the Virtues of Black Womanhood.* Cleveland: Pilgrim Press, 2000.

Wimbush, Vincent, ed. *African Americans and the Bible: Sacred Texts and Social Structures.* New York: Continuum, 2001.

Black Catholics

Black Bishops of the United States. *What We Have Seen and Heard.* Cincinnati: St. Anthony Messenger Press, 1984.

Brown, Joseph. *To Stand on the Rock: Meditations on Black Catholic Identity*. Maryknoll, NY: Orbis Books, 1998.

Copeland, M. Shawn. *Enfleshing Freedom: Body, Race, and Being*. Minneapolis: Fortress Press, 2010.

————, ed. *Uncommon Faithfulness: The Black Catholic Experience*. Maryknoll, NY: Orbis Books, 2009.

Davis, Cyprian. *The History of Black Catholics in the United States*. New York: Crossroad, 1990.

————, and Jamie Phelps, eds. *Stamped with the Image of God: African Americans as God's Image in Black*. Maryknoll, NY: Orbis Books, 2003.

Deggs, Sr. Mary Bernard. *No Cross, No Crown: Black Nuns in Nineteenth-Century New Orleans*. Bloomington: Indiana University Press, 2002.

Dolan, Jay P. *Catholic Revivalism: The American Experience: 1830–1900*. Notre Dame, IN: Univeristy of Notre Dame Press, 1978.

Hayes, Diana L., and Cyprian Davis, OSB. *Taking Down Our Harps: Black Catholics in the United States*. Maryknoll, NY: Orbis Books, 1999.

Massingale, Bryan N. *Racial Justice and the Catholic Church*. Maryknoll, NY: Orbis Books, 2010.

Murphy, Thomas. *Jesuit Slaveholding in Maryland, 1717–1838*. New York: Routledge, 2001.

Phelps, Jamie T., OP. *Black and Catholic: The Challenge and Gift of Black Folk*. Milwaukee: Marquette University Press, 1997.

Black Liberation Theology

Cleage, Albert. *The Black Messiah*. Kansas City: Sheed and Ward, 1968.

Cone, James H. *Black Theology and Black Power*. New York: Seabury Press, 1969; Maryknoll, NY: Orbis Books, 1997.

————. *A Black Theology of Liberation*. Philadelphia: Lippincott, 1970; Maryknoll, NY: Orbis Books, 2010.

————. *God of the Oppressed*. New York: Seabury Press, 1975; Maryknoll, NY: Orbis Books, 1997.

————. *The Spirituals and the Blues*. Maryknoll, NY: Orbis Books, 1992.

Evans, Jr., James H. *We Have Been Believers*. Minneapolis: Fortress Press, 1992.

————. *We Shall All Be Changed: Social Problems and Theological Renewal*. Minneapolis: Fortress Press, 2008.

Wilmore, Gayraud S. *Black Religion and Black Radicalism: An Interpretation of the Religious History of Afro-American People*. 2nd edition, revised and enlarged. Maryknoll, NY: Orbis Books, 1983.

Womanist Theology/Spirituality

Cannon, Katie G. *Black Womanist Ethics*. Atlanta, GA: Scholars Press, 1988.

Copeland, M. Shawn. *Enfleshing Freedom: Body, Race, and Being*. Minneapolis: Fortress Press, 2010.

Douglas, Kelly Brown. *The Black Christ*. Maryknoll, NY: Orbis Books, 1994.

————. *What's Faith Got to Do with It?: Black Bodies, Christian Souls*. Maryknoll, NY: Orbis Books, 2005.

Grant, Jacqueline. *White Woman's Christ, Black Woman's Jesus*. Atlanta, GA: Scholars Press, 1989.

Hayes, Diana L. *Hagar's Daughters: Womanist Ways of Being in the World*. Mahwah, NJ: Paulist Press, 1995.

————. *Standing in the Shoes My Mother Made: Womanist Theology*. Minneapolis: Fortress Press, 2010.

Terrell, JoAnne Marie. *Power in the Blood: The Cross in the African American Experience*. Maryknoll, NY: Orbis Books, 1998.

Townes, Emilie. *In a Blaze of Glory: Womanist Spirituality as Social Witness*. Nashville, TN: Abingdon Press, 1995.

Walker, Alice. *In Search of Our Mothers' Gardens: Womanist Prose*. New York: Harcourt Brace Jovanovich, 1983.

Williams, Delores S. *Sisters in the Wilderness: Womanist Theology*. Maryknoll, NY: Orbis Books, 1995.

Index

Africa: American regard for, 9–10; common belief systems of, 15–16; daughters of, 138; diversity in, 11; orality of culture, 42; religious systems of, 11–13. *See also* African traditional religion

African Americans: African heritage of, 1–2; bodies of, Christianity's role in humanizing and dehumanizing, 158–61; conservatism of, in the early twentieth century, 107; desiring true physical and spiritual freedom, 112–13; development of, 2–3; establishing churches, 90–91, 93; identity of, reflected in their naming, 131, 186, 191n2; mature in their faith, 187; moving to non-Christian faiths, 186; paradoxical faith of, 68, 72; passivity of, 75; questioning their faith, 119; racial heritage of, 10–11; self-understanding of, 9; story of, told in their spirituality, 5; subversive presence of, 189; transformed from Africans, 68; yearning for an understanding of themselves and God, 10

African American spirituality: African American women's spiri-

tuality, 58 (*See also* womanist theology); African resources found in, 181; alternate forms of, 107–8; characteristics of, 3–5, 122, 123; complexity of, 80; defining and delineating, 170–71; different from that of white U.S. Christians, 50; forging of, 2; grounded in devotion to the Holy Spirit, 4; liberating nature of, 131; linking to African spirituality, 91; as pragmatic spirituality, 181–83; as quest for communion with God, 174; resulting from a people's encounter with God, 2–3; rooted in slave experience, 50–51; as spirituality of resistance, 158; as spiritual matrix, 159–60; survival of, 49, 189; transformation of, 136. *See also* Black church; Black religion

African culture, providing origins for African American spirituality, 9–11

African Episcopal Church, 98

Africanisms, in the U.S., 31–34, 38–39

African Methodist Episcopal Church, 98, 207n13

African Methodist Episcopal Zion Church, 98

219